Practice-Oriented Study Guide for Research Methods for Social Work

Allen Rubin
University of Texas at Austin

Brooks/Cole Publishing Company
I(T)P® An International Thomson Publishing Company

Pacific Grove • Albany • Belmont • Bonn • Boston • Cincinnati • Detroit • Johannesburg • London
Madrid • Melbourne • Mexico City • New York • Paris • Singapore • Tokyo • Toronto • Washington

To My Wonderful Sisters and Brother-in-Law
Corrine and Morley Harris
Leah Lambert

Sponsoring Editor: *Lisa Gebo*
Marketing Team: *Jean Thompson, Deborah Petit*
Editorial Assistant: *Terry Thomas*
Production Coordination: *The Book Company*
Production Editor: *Jamie Sue Brooks*
Manuscript Editor: *Elizabeth Judd*
Permissions Editor: *Carline Haga*
Cover and Interior Design: *Donna Davis*
Typesetting: *The Cowans*
Cover Printing: *Edwards Brothers*
Printing and Binding: *Edwards Brothers*

For more information, contact:

BROOKS/COLE PUBLISHING COMPANY
511 Forest Lodge Road
Pacific Grove, CA 93950
USA

International Thomson Publishing Europe
Berkshire House 168–173
High Holborn
London WC1V 7AA
England

Thomas Nelson Australia
102 Dodds Street
South Melbourne, 3205
Victoria, Australia

Nelson Canada
1120 Birchmount Road
Scarborough, Ontario
Canada M1K 5G4

International Thomson Editores
Seneca 53
Col. Polanco
11560 México D. F. México

International Thomson Publishing GmbH
Königswinterer Strasse 418
53227 Bonn
Germany

International Thomson Publishing Asia
221 Henderson Road
#05–10 Henderson Building
Singapore 0315

International Thomson Publishing Japan
Hirakawacho Kyowa Building, 3F
2-2-1 Hirakawacho
Chiyoda-ku, Tokyo 102
Japan

Printed in the United States of America.

10 9 8 7 6 5 4 3 2 1

Library of Congress Cataloging-in-Publication Data

Rubin, Allen.
Practice-oriented study guide for Research methods for social work / Allen Rubin.
p. cm.
"For use in conjunction with the third ed. of Research methods for social work, by Allen Rubin and Earl Babbie"—Pref.
ISBN 0-534-34498-4
1. Social service—Research—Methodology—Outlines, syllabi, etc.
I. Rubin, Allen. Research methods for social work. II. Title.
HV11.R82 1997
361'.0072—dc20 96-31385
CIP

Contents

PART 1 AN INTRODUCTION TO INQUIRY

Chapter 1 Human Inquiry and Science 1
Chapter 2 Theory and Research 11
Chapter 3 The Ethics and Politics of Social Work Research 20

PART 2 PROBLEM FORMULATION AND MEASUREMENT

Chapter 4 Problem Formulation 32
Chapter 5 Conceptualization and Operationalization 42
Chapter 6 Measurement 49
Chapter 7 Constructing Measurement Instruments 61

PART 3 THE LOGIC OF RESEARCH DESIGN

Chapter 8 The Logic of Sampling 70
Chapter 9 Causal Inference and Group Designs 87
Chapter 10 Single-Subject Designs 102

PART 4 QUANTITATIVE AND QUALITATIVE MODES OF OBSERVATION

Chapter 11 Survey Research 116
Chapter 12 Qualitative Research Methods 123
Chapter 13 Unobtrusive Research: Quantitative and Qualitative Methods 134

PART 5 ANALYSIS OF DATA

Chapter 14 Processing Data 144
Chapter 15 Interpreting Descriptive Statistics and Tables 151
Chapter 16 Inferential Data Analysis: Part 1 162
Chapter 17 Inferential Data Analysis: Part 2 174

PART 6 THE SOCIAL CONTEXT OF RESEARCH

Chapter 18 Program Evaluation 187

ANSWERS TO REVIEW QUESTIONS 202

PREFACE

This *Study Guide* is designed for use in conjunction with the third edition of *Research Methods for Social Work,* by Allen Rubin and Earl Babbie. Its purpose is to enhance your comprehension of the material in the text, with a major focus on applying that material to problems that you may be likely to encounter in your social work practice.

Each chapter will correspond to the chapter of the same number in the Rubin and Babbie text, and will begin with the major objectives of that chapter from the standpoint of the main points that a practitioner should know in applying the material to practice. You may want to examine the objectives before reading the chapter, not only to prepare you to better understand the chapter, but also to see its relevance to practice. Knowing in advance how research methods material can be applied to practice may make the material more relevant and interesting to you, and therefore easier to learn.

The same could be said for the chapter summary that follows the objectives. The summary will also focus on practice applications. In addition to reading the summary before you read the chapter of the text, you may want to reread it afterward, to improve your understanding of the material.

After you have read the chapter and reread the summary and feel you have a reasonable grasp of the content, you will be ready to answer the review questions that follow the summary. These questions test your knowledge of the material and ability to apply it to social work practice. After you write down your answers to the review questions, you may check their accuracy by examining the correct answers in the Answers to Review Questions at the end of this *Study Guide*. You may want to reexamine the Rubin and Babbie text to improve your understanding of the material relevant to those questions you answered incorrectly. Going through this process may improve your performance on exams, and perhaps your performance as a practitioner as well.

After completing the review questions, you will encounter several brief exercises that give you an opportunity to practice applying the text material for that chapter. In preparing to work on each exercise, it may be helpful to reread the portion of the text chapter that pertains to the concepts you need to understand in order to complete the exercise. You may want to ask your instructor for guidance on which exercises to do and which will be discussed in class.

Finally, at the end of each chapter you will find several discussion questions. These discussion questions may not have a specific "correct" answer, but by writing out your answers, in your own words, you may be better prepared for class discussions of these issues and may better understand these issues, particularly in regard to social work practice applications.

Good luck with your research course. I hope you enjoy it and find it highly relevant to social work practice. If you have any comments on the helpfulness of this *Study Guide,* or suggestions for improving it, I would be delighted to hear from you.

CHAPTER

Human Inquiry and Science

OBJECTIVES

1. Identify examples of how agreement reality and experiential reality can agree or disagree in a social work agency.
2. Provide an example of how a social worker may encounter tradition as a basis for practice knowledge, and discuss the advantages and disadvantages of relying on tradition as a guide to practice.
3. Provide an example of how a social worker may encounter authority as a basis for practice knowledge, and consider the advantages and disadvantages of relying on authority as a guide to practice.
4. Provide examples of how the following errors in personal inquiry can occur in social work practice: inaccurate observation, overgeneralization, selective observation, made-up information, ex post facto hypothesizing, illogical reasoning, ego involvement in understanding, premature closure of inquiry, and mystification.
5. Explain how a scientific approach to social work practice helps safeguard against these errors.
6. Explain why it is important to test social work "practice wisdom" that is generally accepted but not previously tested.
7. Distinguish premodern, modern, and postmodern views of reality.
8. Distinguish the deterministic perspective of human behavior from the freewill perspective.
9. Define probabilistic knowledge, and explain and give a social welfare example of how it fits within a deterministic model of human behavior.
10. Identify limitations of the deterministic model and the implications of that model for legal or moral responsibility.
11. Distinguish idiographic and nomothetic models of understanding human behavior, and give an example of how each model would attempt to develop social work practice knowledge.
12. Contrast and distinguish qualitative methods of social work inquiry from quantitative methods, and provide an example of how each can provide useful information in answering a practice problem that social workers may encounter.

PRACTICE-RELEVANT SUMMARY

Social work practitioners, like everyone else, must deal with two realities in their pursuit of truth. One is *agreement reality.* When you start working in a social work agency, you will find that many or all of the agency staff agree that certain things are true. Often they are correct in their shared beliefs; sometimes they are wrong. The other reality is *experiential reality,* which pertains to things you will learn as a result of your direct experience. It is possible that your experiential reality as a practitioner may lead you to question the agreement reality you encounter, or that the agreement reality shared by others may lead you to question the reality you have experienced.

If you take a scientific approach to your social work practice, your pursuit of truth will not be limited to only one reality. Instead, you will want two criteria to be met. What you do as a practitioner should be guided by both *logic* and *experience.* The experience you rely on may be your own or it may be reported by others in the professional literature. The main point here is that you will have an open mind and not just rely solely on what others tell you is true or what your own experiences lead you to believe as a sufficient guide to your practice.

Early in your practice, you will understandably rely heavily on two important sources of knowledge to guide your practice: tradition and authority. Relying on *tradition* involves conforming to an agency's traditionally preferred ways of doing things. Relying on *authority* means considering the reputed expertise of the source of the information in deciding whether to be guided by that information. Tradition and authority are double-edged swords in the search for practice knowledge. They provide inexperienced practitioners with a starting point, but they are sometimes wrong. Relying on them too heavily can impede your openness to finding flaws in the transmitted practice wisdom and, consequently, to finding better ways to practice.

Common errors in your own inquiry into practice knowledge—errors that also might be committed by others in your agency who are transmitting flawed knowledge—include inaccurate observation, overgeneralization, selective observation, made-up information, ex post facto hypothesizing, illogical reasoning, ego involvement in understanding, premature closure of inquiry, and mystification. *Inaccurate observation* occurs when we are too casual in our observations, not making deliberate attempts to reduce errors. *Overgeneralization* occurs when our generalizations are based on an insufficient number of observations. *Selective observation* occurs when we look for things that match our predilections and ignore things that don't match them. *Made-up information* refers to a process in which we think up reasons to explain away inconsistencies between what we believe and what we observe. For example, when research results fail to support the effectiveness of our favorite interventions, we may say that the tested intervention was not implemented properly. In a similar vein, *ex post facto hypothesizing* occurs when we go fishing for reasons to explain away discrepancies between observations and beliefs. We also may use *illogical reasoning* to explain away inconsistencies between observations and beliefs, such as when we say that the exception proves the rule. *Ego involvement* can lead to error when we resist accepting observations that make us look less desirable. The *premature closure of inquiry* occurs when we rule out certain lines of inquiry that might produce findings that we would find undesirable. *Mystification* occurs when we attribute things we don't understand to supernatural or mystical causes—such as when we assert that a cherished belief about practice effectiveness must be true and is beyond the ability of researchers to test out.

In taking a scientific approach to social work practice, some of the things we can do to help safeguard against these errors include: insisting that all knowledge and beliefs are open to question and to change, engaging in an ongoing process of testing and retesting our beliefs, consciously and systematically ensuring careful observation, replicating observations across many cases, comparing the observations made by independent observers, and striving for objectivity.

In light of the foregoing errors, and in taking a scientific approach to social work practice, it is important to test social work "practice wisdom" that is generally accepted but not previously tested. Research has found that some interventions that used to be generally accepted as effective are actually ineffective and perhaps harmful.

The *deterministic perspective* on human behavior sees human behavior as a result of prior causes, which themselves result from even earlier causes. This differs from the *freewill perspective,* which views human behavior as the product of personal decisions, or willpower. Because so many factors influence human behavior, and because each person tends to be exposed to a myriad of factors in unique ways, the deterministic model seeks probabilistic knowledge—knowledge that presupposes that people exposed to particular factors are more or less likely to behave in particular ways than are people not exposed to those factors.

The deterministic model of human behavior has some limitations. It does not absolve individuals of legal or moral responsibility. It recognizes that it is hard to find the causes of many human phenomena and that causal patterns are not simple. The model also is complicated by the influence of current situations on human behavior. Behaviors that seem to be occurring simultaneously can be shaping each other. Moreover, the anticipation of future events can influence current behaviors before the future events occur. The fact that our percerption of current or future events can shape our current behavior does not necessarily undermine the deterministic model, but it can make it extremely difficult to determine what is the cause and what is the effect.

There are two models for attempting to study and understand the causes of human behavior. The *idiographic model* aims at explanation by seeking to understand everything about a particular case, using as many causative factors as possible. The *nomothetic model* tries to generalize to populations in probabilistic terms about the most important causative factors for a general phenomenon studied across a large number of cases.

Not all social work researchers share the same philosophical assumptions. Some question determinism. Some even doubt whether an objective external reality exists, arguing instead that there are only multiple subjective realities. Differences in philosophical assumptions can lead to differences over preferred research methods. Two overarching types of research methods that have been the focus of much debate in the recent social work literature are quantitative methods and qualitative methods. *Quantitative methods* emphasize the need to be precise, to verify hypotheses, to determine causality, and to come up with findings that can be analyzed statistically and generalized. *Qualitative methods* are less likely to involve numbers and are less concerned with precision, generalization, or testing out what really causes what. Instead, qualitative methods try to tap deeper, subjective meanings and generate tentative new insights or new hypotheses. Although some have argued about these two research approaches in ways that imply they are in competition with one another and are inherently incompatible, many others view them as playing an equally important and complementary role in building social work knowledge. Some of the best research studies have combined qualitative and quantitative methods.

Regardless of which research approach is used, researchers would like to believe that their findings are true and are not just a reflection of their own subjective biases. However, objectivity is not easy to achieve. Some would argue that no research is free of biases. Researchers want their findings to be important, and this desire can predispose them toward unintentionally interpreting their findings in distorted ways. When you conduct or read research studies, one of your chief concerns should be whether the way the research is conducted provides safeguards to prevent the researcher's biases from influencing the nature of the data gathered and how they are interpreted. Much of this book is about how you can provide those safeguards or determine whether others have done so.

REVIEW QUESTIONS

1. Social work practitioners make decisions based on:
   a. Tradition
   b. Authority
   c. Agreement reality
   d. Their experience
   e. All of the above

2. A social work practitioner disregards the findings of research studies indicating that Intervention A is ineffective with her agency's clientele and that Intervention B is more effective. Instead, she uses Intervention A because her supervisor recommends it and all the other practitioners in the agency have been using it for years. This is an example of:
   a. Tradition
   b. Authority
   c. Experiential reality
   d. The scientific method
   e. All of the above
   f. Only a and b

3. A social worker attends a workshop on culturally sensitive practice, where he is told that frail elderly Asian Americans are more likely to be well cared for by their extended families than are their white counterparts. Therefore, when he is shortly thereafter assigned to provide services to a frail elderly Korean woman, he assumes that her extended family is caring for her adequately. This is an example of:
   a. Scientific practice
   b. Relying on authority
   c. Overgeneralization
   d. All of the above
   e. Only b and c

4. The above social worker later learns that the client was not cared for adequately by her extended family, and therefore concludes that what he was told at the workshop was wrong. This is an example of:
   a. Scientific practice
   b. Logical reasoning
   c. Overgeneralization
   d. Only a and b

5. A social work practitioner has attended several costly continuing education workshops that have given her advanced expertise and a great reputation in delivering a new intervention. Five equally rigorous studies that evaluate the effectiveness of the intervention are published. Four conclude it is worthless; one concludes it is effective. The social worker dismisses the four studies indicating the intervention is worthless as poor research without even reading them carefully and concludes that the study supporting the intervention is the only decent study. This is an example of:
   a. Scientific practice
   b. Selective observation
   c. Ego involvement
   d. Overgeneralization
   e. Both b and c are correct

6. The prediction or observation that abused children are more likely than nonabused children to become perpetrators of abuse is an example of:
   a. Probabilistic reasoning
   b. A relationship
   c. Independent and dependent variables
   d. All of the above

7. Acceptance of a deterministic model of human behavior:
   a. Implies absolving individuals of legal or moral responsibility for their behavior
   b. Means attributing events to one cause
   c. Implies assuming simple causal patterns apply to most people
   d. All of the above
   e. None of the above

8. Which of the following statements is *not* true regarding objectivity and subjectivity in scientific inquiry?
   a. Both quantitative and qualitative methods seek to attain objectivity.
   b. Researchers have no vested interests in finding certain results.
   c. We can assume objectivity has been achieved when different observers, with different vested interests, agree.
   d. None of the above; all are true.

9. Which of the following is not true about quantitative and qualitative methods?
   a. Quantitative methods emphasize precision and generalizable statistical findings.
   b. Qualitative methods emphasize deeper meanings, using observations not easily reduced to numbers.
   c. The two methods are incompatible and cannot be combined in the same study.
   d. Which type of method to emphasize depends on the conditions and purposes of the inquiry.
   e. None of the above; all are true.

10. A study of a particular homeless family that seeks to understand everything about that particular family and all the causes for its homelessness would exemplify:
    a. The idiographic model
    b. The nomothetic model
    c. Postmodernism
    d. Probabilistic reasoning

11. A study of a large number of homeless families that seeks to generalize about the most important factors causing homelessness across the entire population would exemplify:
    a. The idiographic model
    b. The nomothetic model
    c. Postmodernism
    d. Subjective inquiry

EXERCISE 1.1

In social work practice we continually must make quick decisions based on limited information. Consequently, we must learn to accept the fact that we occasionally will make errors, or at least think of better ways of handling a situation after it is too late. Sometimes we make the right decision for the wrong reasons; sometimes we make wrong decisions that nonetheless seemed logical and justifiable at the time. Recall a decision you have made or observed in your practice experience (or field practicum) that was flawed because it was based exclusively on tradition or authority or because it reflected one of the following errors of human inquiry: inaccurate observation, overgeneralization, selective observation, or ego involvement in understanding. (If you have had insufficient social work experience to come up with an example from your own practice, recall a flawed decision from your other life experiences.)

1. Describe the decision.

2. Explain how it reflected one of the problems listed above and described in Chapter 1.

3. Discuss how a scientific approach may have improved the decision.

EXERCISE 1.2

1. Suppose you are a direct service practitioner and your clients are perpetrators of abuse, such as juvenile sex offenders or abusive parents. Write a brief essay on how you would be able to hold a deterministic view of their abusive behaviors while at the same time holding them legally and morally responsible for those behaviors.

2. Based on your essay, what could you say to your clients that would convey the potential for forgiveness and redemption, while still conveying the need to accept responsibility for their behavior?

EXERCISE 1.3

Suppose you are providing services to an adolescent boy who is depressed and withdrawn and to his mother, who tends to speak for him instead of letting him speak for himself. Explain how the deterministic model can be applied to this case, and identify the complexities in applying it in light of social systems dynamics and the person-in-environment framework.

EXERCISE 1.4

Select a problem of concern to social work practitioners. Describe how it would be studied differently depending on whether the idiographic or nomothetic model of understanding guides the inquiry.

DISCUSSION QUESTIONS

1. Suppose you are a child therapist in a child guidance center, where you provide play therapy. You learn of one play therapy approach that is nondirective and another that is directive. Discuss how you would utilize tradition and authority in deciding which approach to use. Discuss the problems in relying exclusively on tradition and authority as your guide.

2. Suppose you have invested a great deal of time and money to attend workshops to obtain special, advanced expertise in a promising new intervention approach that none of your colleagues is trained to provide. Suppose you decide to learn for yourself, through your experiential reality in providing the intervention, whether it seems to be more effective than alternative approaches in helping clients. Discuss the errors in personal inquiry to which you would be vulnerable. Discuss some ways that a scientific inquiry about the effectiveness of the intervention would help safeguard against those errors.

CHAPTER

Theory and Research

OBJECTIVES

1. Describe how theory is used as part of scientifically oriented social work practice.
2. Provide an example to illustrate the links between theory and research.
3. Describe the parallel functions of theory in social work practice and research.
4. Provide examples to illustrate how four different social work practice models could influence the way a social work research question is posed or studied.
5. Define the term *paradigm* and describe how different paradigms could influence research.
6. Provide examples to illustrate how social work researchers guided by the interpretivist or conflict paradigms would go about investigating a social work research question differently than researchers guided by the positivist or post-positivist paradigm.
7. Distinguish theory from paradigms, philosophy, or belief.
8. Define and compare deductive and inductive logic.
9. Illustrate how inductive and deductive logic are used in scientifically oriented social work practice.
10. Give four examples of social work practice variables, list their respective attributes, and explain the difference between a variable and an attribute.
11. Give an example of a possible relationship between practice variables.
12. Identify the independent and dependent variables in the above relationship.

PRACTICE-RELEVANT SUMMARY

Just as some practitioners conduct their practice giving little thought to theory, some research studies are conducted with no links to theory. An example of the former may be practitioners who act on impulse, perhaps unconsciously reacting to unresolved issues in their own lives. An example of the latter may be an administrator who thoughtlessly manipulates masses of agency data searching unsystematically for some descriptive fact that will make the agency look good. Once obtaining that finding, the administrator may disseminate it to board members or funding sources—for public relations purposes only—with no attempts to pursue the meaning of the finding further or to use it to improve understanding. Ideally, however, both practice and research should be closely linked to theory (as well as to each other).

Linkage to theory can come in two forms: inductive and deductive. Using the *deductive model*, we move from the general to the particular. We start with a general theory as our guide, next develop hypotheses based on the theory, and then make observations of operationalized indicators to test that hypothesis. Using the *inductive model*, we move from the particular to the general. We begin with a set of observations, look for patterns in those observations, and attempt to generate hypotheses and theory based on the patterns we observe.

In actual practice, deduction and induction alternate. We may inductively generate hypotheses and then deductively test them, or we may deductively test hypotheses and then inductively seek to better understand our results by conducting a new set of observations.

The basic building blocks of theories are called *concepts*. Concepts are abstract elements representing classes of phenomena. To research a specific concept, we must select its operationalized indicators—that is, we must specify how the concept will be observed. The operationalized indicators of concepts are called *variables*. In constructing theories, we look for relationships among concepts, and in research we look for relationships among variables. When we specify expected relationships among variables, we are formulating *hypotheses*. These hypotheses can be tested to see if they are supported empirically. If they are empirically supported, then the theory is supported. But a disorganized pile of concepts, observations, and relationships do not make up a theory. The theory's components must be connected to each other logically and must coalesce to help explain related phenomena.

Variables that cause or explain something are called *independent variables*, and variables that are explained by or are the effects of the independent variable are called *dependent variables*. Variables are logical groupings of attributes. *Attributes* are characteristics. Gender, for example, is a variable composed of the attributes male and female.

Social work practice and research are guided by *practice models* that synthesize social science theories. The way research questions are posed or studied will be influenced by the practice model guiding the investigator. The same can be said about the influence of *paradigms*, which are fundamental models or schemes that organize our view of the world. Researchers guided by *positivist* or *postpositivist paradigms* emphasize objectivity, precision, and generalizability in their inquiries. Researchers guided by the *interpretivist paradigm* are less concerned with precision and generalizability and more interested in probing deeper into the subjective meanings of human experience. *Conflict paradigm* researchers use a variety of methods employed by researchers following other paradigms, but they are distinguished by their rejection of scientific neutrality and objectivity and their mission to interpret findings through the filter of their empowerment and advocacy aims.

REVIEW QUESTIONS

1. Which of the following is the *best* example of a hypothesis that might be held by a social worker providing a support group to caregivers of relatives with AIDS?

a. Compassionate family members should care for their relative with AIDS.

b. The caregivers will feel a considerable degree of stigma.

c. Many caregivers will be in denial.

d. Participation in the support group will reduce caregivers' levels of depression.

2. Which of the following approaches to scientific inquiry can be used commonly by a social work practitioner?

   a. Deductive reasoning

   b. Inductive reasoning

   c. Both inductive and deductive reasoning

   d. Reductionistic reasoning

3. A practitioner notices on three successive occasions when her client—a teenage girl in joint custody—has visited her father for the weekend, she seems more depressed and anxious. The practitioner then wonders whether there is something about the father's behavior, or the father-daughter relationship, that is contributing to the depression and anxiety. This is an example of:

   a. Inductive reasoning

   b. Deductive reasoning

   c. Both inductive and deductive reasoning

   d. Reductionistic reasoning

4. According to Rubin and Babbie, which of the following statements about practice models for social work practice is *not* true?

   a. They tend to be based on the synthesis of existing theories.

   b. They are mutually exclusive; they do not overlap.

   c. They get reinterpreted over time, in a manner that may broaden them but blur their distinctions.

   d. They can influence how we choose to research social work problems.

5. A paradigm is a:

   a. Frame of reference for interpreting the world

   b. Theory

   c. Law

   d. Concept

6. A social work supervisor, trained in and oriented to psychoanalysis, notices that her supervisee has a high rate of premature terminations. She recommends that

he attend more continuing education workshops on object relations theory and decides to measure whether his treatment completion rate increases after he attends the workshops. This is an example of:

a. Primarily inductive reasoning
b. Primarily deductive reasoning
c. Both inductive and deductive reasoning equally
d. The functionalist practice model

7. Scientific practitioners using the working principle of intersubjectivity would:
   a. Inquire as to whether the view of reality expressed by one member of the client system is also expressed by other members
   b. Attempt to be subjective
   c. Endorse the notion that no objective reality exists
   d. Do research on many subjects

8. If we postulate that witnessing parental violence increases the likelihood of behavioral problems in children, then:
   a. Whether a child witnesses parental violence is the independent variable.
   b. Whether a child develops behavioral problems is the dependent variable.
   c. Both a and b are correct.
   d. Neither a nor b is correct.

9–11: Suppose we predict that social service consumers in urban regions are more likely to prematurely terminate services than consumers in rural regions, while the latter are more likely to complete services.

9. In the above example, "urban region" would be
   a. An attribute
   b. A variable
   c. A relationship

10. In the above example, "region" would be
   a. An attribute
   b. A variable
   c. A relationship

11. In the above example, "service completers" would be
   a. An attribute
   b. A variable
   c. A relationship

12. A researcher who hangs out with a small group of homeless people to develop an in-depth subjective understanding of their lives is being guided by what paradigm?

    a. Positivism
    b. Postpositivism
    c. Interpretivism
    d. Conflict paradigm

EXERCISE 2.1

1. Suppose two social workers are co-therapists providing play therapy with a group of preschoolers with conduct disorders. One relies on a behaviorist practice model rooted in learning theory and the principles of operant conditioning. The other relies on a developmental practice model, rooted in notions of providing a nondirective atmosphere where children can work on developmental tasks. Give examples of how each practice model might influence the practitioners to look for different indicators of the quality of the therapeutic process.

2. Suppose you wanted to evaluate the effectiveness of the above play therapy group. Give examples of how the outcome indicators of effectiveness that you choose to examine may differ depending on whether you were guided by a psychosocial practice model versus a behaviorist practice model.

EXERCISE 2.2

In the deductive model of science, the scientist begins with an interest in some aspect of reality, develops a hypothesis based on theory, and tests it through careful, objective observation of specific indicators. Illustrate how social work practitioners providing direct services or working at the macro level go through an analogous process.

EXERCISE 2.3

Specify two possible relationships relevant to social work practice. Identify the independent and dependent variable in each hypothesis, and describe the attributes of each variable.

DISCUSSION QUESTIONS

1. Discuss, using a specific illustration, how a social work practitioner can use both inductive and deductive logic in working with a particular case, community, or organization.

2. Identify a particular practice model with which you closely identify. Discuss how that practice model might help and hinder your practice decisions and your effectiveness as a social work practitioner.

3. Discuss how the practice model you explored in question 2 could influence the kinds of research questions you might choose to investigate.

4. If you were to conduct social work research, do you think you would be most influenced by the positivist, postpositivist, interpretivist, or conflict paradigm? Why?

CHAPTER

The Ethics and Politics of Social Work Research

OBJECTIVES

1. Illustrate the ethical issues involved in the norm of voluntary participation and informed consent, including an example of a hypothetical study in which some practitioners or researchers might reasonably argue that violation of that norm is justified.
2. Illustrate through an example how a noble social worker might conduct a study that unintentionally violates the ethical norm of no harm to participants.
3. Define and distinguish between the ethical norms of anonymity and confidentiality in social work research.
4. Provide two examples of how a social work research study might violate the ethical norm regarding deceiving subjects. One example should be clearly unjustified, and one should be arguable.
5. Describe and illustrate how a social work researcher could unjustifiably violate ethical norms in analysis and reporting.
6. Describe and illustrate the ethical dilemma regarding the right to receive services versus the responsibility to evaluate service effectiveness.
7. Discuss the ethical obligations of social work practitioners to support research in the field.
8. Identify codes in the NASW Code of Ethics relating to how practitioners violate practice ethics if they refuse to participate in, contribute to, or utilize social work research.
9. Identify which ethical principles were violated in the three examples of ethical controversies presented in Chapter 3, and discuss the dilemmas debated in each.
10. Describe the function of institutional review boards.
11. Illustrate how a social work research study could be biased or insensitive regarding gender or culture, and identify steps that can be taken to try to avoid that bias or insensitivity.
12. Identify two ways in which ethical concerns regarding research can be distinguished from political concerns.
13. Illustrate how values and ideology can influence the research process.

14. Discuss why some believe that social work research is never really value-free, and describe contrasting perspectives of what researchers should therefore do in light of the influence of values.
15. Illustrate how the influence of ideological priorities on social work research can stifle debate and ultimately hinder desired social change.

PRACTICE-RELEVANT SUMMARY

Social work research, like social work practice, is guided by codes of ethics. Some of the codes for research parallel codes for practice, and some of the codes for practice bear on the practitioner's responsibilities vis-à-vis research.

For example, just as practitioners are guided by the principle of client self-determination, researchers should honor the principle of voluntary participation and informed consent by participants. At the same time, just as some practitioners might argue that in some cases the principle of self-determination needs to be violated (such as when clients intend to seriously harm themselves or others), some researchers might argue that in some cases the principle of voluntary participation and informed consent needs to be violated (such as when the study is investigating improper and harmful treatment of clients in institutions).

Another ethical principle—one practitioners and researchers can easily agree on—is that participants (or clients) should not be harmed by the research (or intervention). And yet sometimes the harm can be subtle or hard to anticipate, such as when survey respondents are asked about disturbing, unpopular, or demeaning behaviors, characteristics, or attitudes.

One ethical code that research clearly shares with practice is the protection of the subject's (client's) identity. Confidentiality means that the researcher or practitioner knows who said or did what but promises not to reveal their identity. In some research studies it is possible to go a step further, by assuring anonymity. Anonymity prevents even the researcher from identifying a given response with a given respondent. Sometimes it is possible to assure anonymity to research participants, and sometimes it is not. Confidentiality, however, should always be protected. The only exception to this dictum occurs when we learn that a client or subject is being abused or is at imminent risk of seriously harming themself or others. Subjects need to be informed of this possibility as part of the informed consent process before they agree to participate in a study.

Deceiving subjects about the researcher's identity or research purposes is another important ethical concern, one that frequently poses a dilemma. Although it is often useful and even necessary to identify one's research purposes, sometimes the nature of the study requires that these purposes be concealed. In some studies it may be possible to justify using deception on the grounds that there is no other way to do the study and in light of the study's humanitarian value. In other studies this justification may not be convincing. If the use of deception is justified, subjects should be debriefed after the study. Also, as with all ethical guidelines, no study should be conducted without the approval of a human subjects committee that confirms the researcher's belief that the benefits of a study outweigh its risks.

Ethical concerns exist even after a study is completed and its findings are about to be reported. Researchers are obliged to inform readers of the study's technical shortcomings as well as its negative findings. They are also obliged not to portray accidental findings as if they resulted from a carefully preplanned analysis.

Perhaps the most practice-relevant ethical dilemma has to do with the right to receive services versus the responsibility to evaluate service effectiveness. Does our professional responsibility to ensure that the services we provide have been scientifically tested for beneficial or harmful effects justify withholding services from some clients so as to compare experimentally the outcomes for those who receive services and those who don't? This dilemma is easiest to resolve when alternative services can be compared (rather than denying service to one group), when limited resources require placing clients on waiting lists, or when withholding services from clients experiencing a serious crisis would endanger them.

Several studies in social work and allied fields have gained notoriety in connection to ethical issues. In the famous Tuskegee syphilis study, a social worker exposed ethical violations involving the deception and harming of poor African American men suffering from syphilis, who were told they would receive free treatment for the disease when in fact the researchers had no intention of treating it. Instead, they were merely studying the progress of the disease. Stanley Milgram's social psychological laboratory studies of obedience to authority have been criticized for causing psychological suffering among participants who were duped into thinking they were obeying orders to seriously hurt people. Laud Humphreys's study of homosexual acts between strangers meeting in public restrooms was criticized on several grounds, including invasion of privacy and deceiving subjects into thinking he was only a voyeur-participant. A social worker, William Epstein, almost had his professional membership revoked when he duped editors and reviewers of professional journals with a bogus article that he submitted to test for editor bias in favor of publishing studies whose findings supported social work effectiveness over studies whose findings questioned social work effectiveness. A Texas experiment on the effectiveness of a federal pilot program to wean people from the welfare rolls had to abandon the use of a control group when critics argued that all welfare recipients should have been informed of the study and been given the opportunity to receive the pilot program's medical and child care benefits.

Feminist and minority scholars have expressed ethical concerns about studies that are biased or insensitive regarding gender and culture, arguing that such studies can harm women and minorities by offending them, by not pursuing findings that bear on their needs or ways to help them, and by inappropriately generalizing to them. Numerous guidelines have been offered to try to avoid cultural and gender bias and insensitivity in one's research.

There is a fine line between ethical and political issues in social work research. Ethical issues tend to deal more with research methods employed; political issues tend to deal more with how research will be used or its costs. Two common political objections that social workers are likely to encounter regarding proposed research in agencies include the fear that negative findings will hurt agency funding and the fear of bad publicity or lost revenues connected to withholding services in order to establish a control group.

Another source of objections to certain lines of research inquiry is ideologically rooted. Traditionally, scientifically oriented professionals have maintained that one's values, politics, or ideology should not influence one's research. Instead, researchers should strive to maximize objectivity. Recently, however, these notions have come under attack by some scholars who argue that social research is never entirely value-free. Although social work has a long tradition of using research as a tool to achieve ends prescribed by social work values, there is controversy within the profession over whether our values or ideological aims and beliefs should ever take priority over seeking the truth in our research. Research on women or minorities is commonly associated with this controversy, particularly when a study produces, or is apt to produce, findings that may provoke hostility from colleagues who fear that those findings will impede their political or ideological aims.

REVIEW QUESTIONS

1. A social work professor conducts a study to see if students become more tolerant in their attitudes about gay and lesbian issues during the semester. The professor distributes questionnaires, then leaves the room, assuring students that completing the questionnaire is voluntary and that they may return it anonymously via campus mail. Most students do not respond; those who do are the ones most deeply committed to issues of gay and lesbian rights. This illustrates:
   a. Adhering to the guideline of voluntary participation
   b. The conflict between the ethical concern for voluntary participation and the scientific goal of generalizability
   c. Ethical concern with the protection of identity
   d. All of the above
   e. Only a and b

2. Bill and Sarah, two agency social workers, mail client satisfaction questionnaires to agency clientele, requesting their anonymous responses about what they do and do not like about the services they are receiving. Bill and Sarah enter code numbers on each return envelope so they will know who returned the questionnaire and will thus be able to identify clients who did not respond to the survey, for the purposes of follow-up mailings. What ethical principle(s) are Bill and Sarah violating?
   a. Confidentiality
   b. Anonymity
   c. Deceiving subjects
   d. All of the above
   e. Only a and b
   f. Only b and c

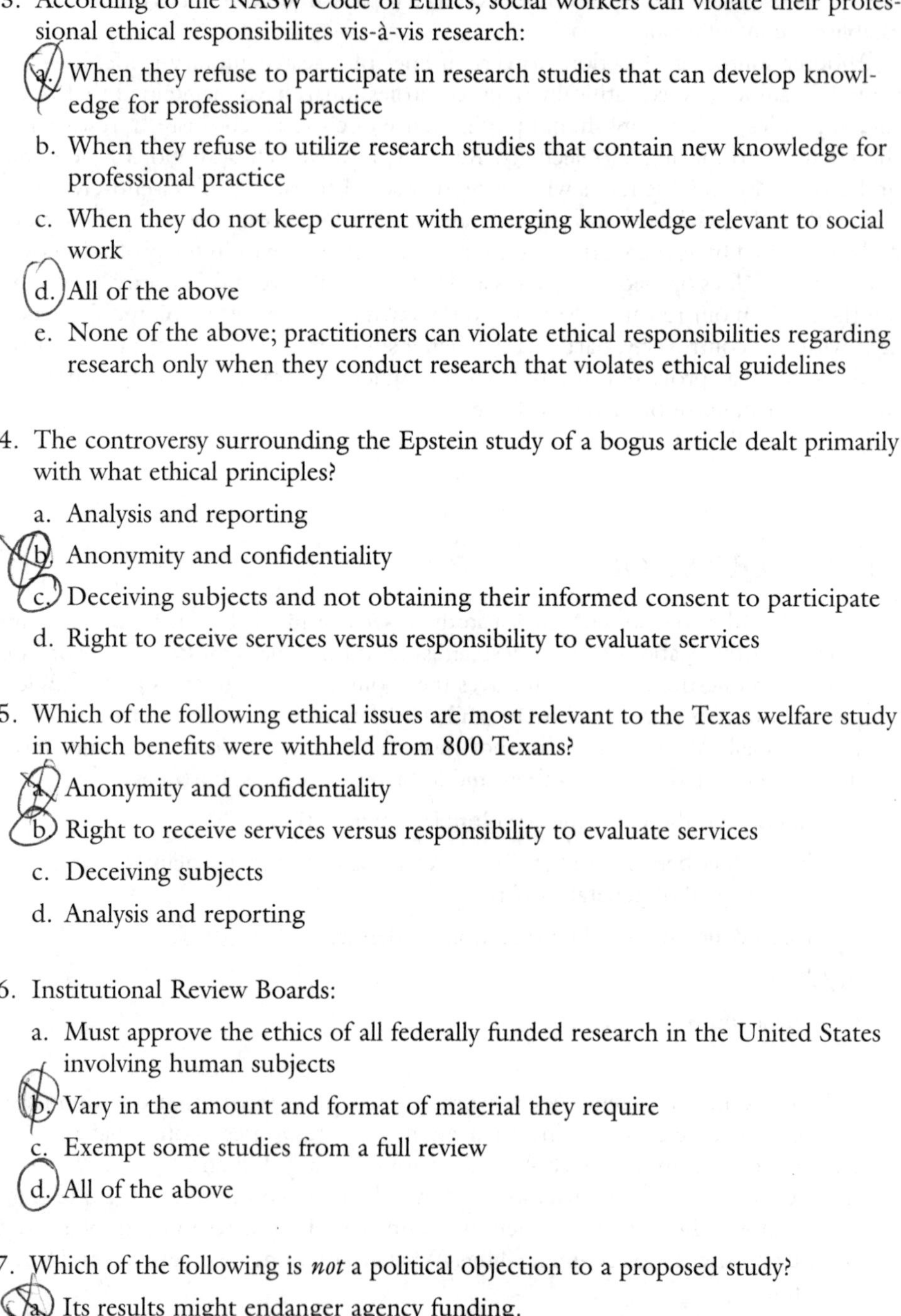

3. According to the NASW Code of Ethics, social workers can violate their professional ethical responsibilites vis-à-vis research:
   a. When they refuse to participate in research studies that can develop knowledge for professional practice
   b. When they refuse to utilize research studies that contain new knowledge for professional practice
   c. When they do not keep current with emerging knowledge relevant to social work
   d. All of the above
   e. None of the above; practitioners can violate ethical responsibilities regarding research only when they conduct research that violates ethical guidelines

4. The controversy surrounding the Epstein study of a bogus article dealt primarily with what ethical principles?
   a. Analysis and reporting
   b. Anonymity and confidentiality
   c. Deceiving subjects and not obtaining their informed consent to participate
   d. Right to receive services versus responsibility to evaluate services

5. Which of the following ethical issues are most relevant to the Texas welfare study in which benefits were withheld from 800 Texans?
   a. Anonymity and confidentiality
   b. Right to receive services versus responsibility to evaluate services
   c. Deceiving subjects
   d. Analysis and reporting

6. Institutional Review Boards:
   a. Must approve the ethics of all federally funded research in the United States involving human subjects
   b. Vary in the amount and format of material they require
   c. Exempt some studies from a full review
   d. All of the above

7. Which of the following is *not* a political objection to a proposed study?
   a. Its results might endanger agency funding.
   b. Its procedures would be unpopular among agency staff.
   c. It might harm participants.
   d. Its results might impede the desired aims of an ideological movement.

8. Which of the following is *not* a guideline to avoid cultural bias and insensitivity in research involving minorities?
   a. Immerse yourself in the culture before finalizing your research design.
   b. Involve minority scholars and representatives of minority groups in designing the research.
   c. Use the best instruments you can find from studies not involving minorities, and if those studies found the instruments to be scientifically rigorous, do not change them.
   d. Use minority, and perhaps bilingual, interviewers to interview minority respondents.
   e. Avoid an exclusive focus on the deficits of minorities.
   f. None of the above; all are recommended guidelines for research on minorities.

9. Which of the following is a recommended guideline to avoid gender bias and insensitivity in research?
   a. Assume that if a measurement instrument can be used successfully with one gender, it will be valid for the other gender.
   b. Generalize findings from one gender to the other; assume no differences.
   c. Look for ways in which the findings are the same for men and women; do not look for differences.
   d. All of the above.
   e. None of the above.

10. Which of the following statements is true about research politics and ideology?
    a. All scholars believe that research can be, and ought to be, value-free.
    b. Social work has a long tradition of using research to attain desired values.
    c. All feminists agree that research should not be done if its results could hinder desired political aims of feminists.
    d. Politically rooted taboos against certain lines of inquiry never do a disservice to the people they seek to protect.
    e. Science is untouched by politics.
    f. All of the above.
    g. None of the above.

EXERCISE 3.1

Listed below are several research situations, like some of those noted in the chapter, that you may encounter in your professional practice. Rank order them according to how seriously they violate either the ethical guidelines discussed in this chapter or the social work profession's code of ethics.

a. While parents await their children in the waiting room of a Child Guidance Center, the center's social work staff instructs them to complete a questionnaire on child-rearing attitudes. The staff will use the findings of this study to prepare a proposal for funding for a parent education program.

b. A community organizer decides to observe, interview folks at, and write about a demonstration against a new welfare policy that would force AFDC recipients to work. The demonstration becomes violent; windows are broken and other property is destroyed. Law enforcement officials demand that the organizer identify people observed breaking the law. Rather than risk arrest as an accomplice after the fact, the organizer complies.

c. Social workers in a battered women's program conduct an evaluation of the effectiveness of the services provided by the program, hoping to bring visibility and resources to the program by publishing the findings. The findings, however, unexpectedly indicate the services are not effective. In light of these findings the social workers decide they must not have conducted a proper study of the services that they are convinced are effective, and they decide not to let anyone know about the study.

d. Two social work students with the same field placement in a public child welfare agency decide to do a research class team project involving interviews with abusive parents. They obtain a list of parents reported to their agency for abuse and then contact them with the explanation that they have been selected at random from the general population to take a sampling about child-rearing attitudes. They say this so as to not make the parents defensive in the interviews.

e. Two other social work students decide to do their class research project by observing the nocturnal activities at a shelter for the homeless. The shelter has a limited number of beds and cannot accommodate everyone seeking housing. The two students show up and wait in line early enough to get beds and then watch and record the goings on at night while they pretend to be asleep.

f. A new intervention is touted as an extremely effective, powerful brief therapy for posttraumatic stress disorder among victims of sexual assault. Although sufficient resources exist to provide this treatment to all clients at a rape crisis center, the decision is made to provide it to only half the clients, so its effects can be compared to the effects of the center's routine services.

g. An in-service training director in a family service agency interviews social work staff about their training needs. To test whether they may be trying to look good by saying they know more than they really know, the director asks if they have sufficient understanding about a fictitious intervention modality.

EXERCISE 3.2

1. For each of the above rankings, explain the reason for your rankings and identify the one or two ethical issues most relevant to the situation.

2. Which situations would you consider minor ethical violations? Which would you consider major ethical violations? Why?

EXERCISE 3.3

List each of the major ethical guidelines emphasized in Chapter 3. Beside each briefly describe the purpose of a hypothetical research study that would be valuable to carry out but that would violate that guideline.

EXERCISE 3.4

Referring to Figure 3-2, prepare an informed consent form for the Buckingham study on Living with the Dying, which is described in Chapter 3 of the text.

EXERCISE 3.5

Your agency wants you to conduct a study of recent immigrants to assess their need for services. What steps would you take before implementing any study in order to minimize cultural bias and insensitivity?

EXERCISE 3.6

Make up and describe two hypothetical studies: one in which it would be justified to delay the provision of services to some clients in order to evaluate the services, and one in which that delay would not be justified.

DISCUSSION QUESTIONS

1. Examine the NASW Code of Ethics. Discuss your views on how strongly and clearly the code implies that social work practitioners are unethical if they refuse to participate in social work practice research or if they fail to utilize practice research to guide their practice.

2. Answer the questions raised in the text at the end of the discussion of Epstein's "Bogus Article to Test Journal Bias" asking you what you think about the controversy surrounding that illustration.

3. Answer the questions raised in the text at the end of the discussion of "Welfare Study Withholds Benefits from 800 Texans" asking you what you think about the controversy surrounding that illustration.

4. Discuss why bias and insensitivity regarding gender and culture are considered to be ethical violations. Identify at least five guidelines to avoid gender bias or insensitivity and at least five guidelines to avoid cultural bias or insensitivity.

5. Discuss your view of the ethics and politics of *The Bell Curve*. Were its authors unethical in conducting or reporting the study the way they did? Why or why not? Include in your discussion the issue of political correctness and its implications for scientific inquiry and for finding new ways to improve social welfare.

CHAPTER

Problem Formulation

OBJECTIVES

1. Identify examples of how social work researchers and practitioners follow the same problem-solving process.
2. List each phase of the research process, and explain how phases are interrelated and can loop back to earlier phases.
3. Describe the basic elements of a research proposal.
4. Develop a research question that would be highly relevant to social work practice.
5. Identify some major obstacles to the feasibility of studying the foregoing research question.
6. Identify the functions of a literature review and some major sources you would use in conducting one.
7. Provide an example of an exploratory research topic of value to social work practice, and discuss how the exploratory results might lead to a descriptive or explanatory study.
8. Provide a hypothetical example of a valuable descriptive study and explain how its findings might set the stage for an explanatory or exploratory study.
9. Provide an example of a useful explanatory study and explain how its findings might loop back to the need for more exploratory study.
10. Provide an example of a practice-relevant cross-sectional study, a practice-relevant trend study, a practice-relevant panel study, and a practice-relevant cohort study.
11. Give examples of how a particular research topic could be studied using individuals, groups, or social artifacts as the units of analysis.
12. Provide a hypothetical example of the ecological fallacy in a hypothetical social work research study.

PRACTICE-RELEVANT SUMMARY

Social work researchers and practitioners follow essentially the same problem-solving process. Both begin by formulating a problem. Next they generate, explore, and select alternative strategies for solving the problem. The chosen approach is then implemented and evaluated, and the findings are disseminated. In both practice and research these phases are contingent on one another. Problems encountered at any phase may require looping back to earlier phases and rethinking one's approach. Even the successful completion of the entire process implies the likelihood of looping back, since one's findings are likely to stimulate new ideas about problems or solutions one would like to study.

Researchers seeking funding for their inquiries commonly have to develop a research proposal. Practitioners seeking funds to evaluate their programs may have to do the same. Proposals begin with a statement of the problem or objectives of the study, its importance and timeliness, and how the study is likely to benefit practice and policy. The problem statement should fit the priorities of the funding source. A literature review follows the problem statement. It should be sufficiently inclusive to let funders know you know the literature and to show them how your study builds on the literature, yet it should not be so detailed that it becomes tedious. Next the proposal should describe the subjects for study and the sampling plan, what variables will be measured and how, and data collection methods and data analysis plans. The proposal should conclude with a schedule of the research stages and a budget.

While the elements of research proposals are fairly common, irrespective of the type of research being proposed, proposals for qualitative studies pose a special challenge. Because qualitative inquiry involves less structure and less advance planning of detailed methodological procedures, and because of the unpredictable nature of qualitative research, the qualitative proposal writer encounters the paradox of planning what cannot and should not be planned in advance. The dilemma for the writer, then, is figuring out how to put enough detail about the plan and its possible results in the proposal to enable potential funders to evaluate the merits of the proposal, while at the same time remaining true to the unstructured, flexible, inductive qualitative approach.

In selecting research topics, the impetus should come from the information needs confronting practitioners, administrators, and policymakers attempting to solve practical problems in social welfare, service delivery, or practice. Thus, social work research has an "applied" emphasis, rather than just seeking knowledge for its own sake or solely to satisfy the researcher's idiosyncratic curiosity. The answers to your research questions should be highly relevant to others concerned about social welfare or social work practice.

An important early step in the problem formulation phase involves considering feasibility obstacles to one's research ideas. Common feasibility obstacles include fiscal costs, time constraints, ethical problems, and difficulty obtaining required cooperation from participants and agency administrators and practitioners. Another important early step is the literature review. Although the literature summary in a research proposal may be concise, the researcher should be thoroughly grounded in the literature, which often can ensure that the research questions chosen for study adequately address the burning issues in the field and build on the work of others. Common places to find relevant literature include abstracts, bibliographies, guides, and indexes. Computerized searches may be helpful; another possibility is scanning the tables of contents of recent periodicals.

Research can be for the purpose of exploration, description, and/or explanation. Exploratory studies typically use flexible research methods and are less concerned with producing generalizable facts than with providing a tentative familiarity with a topic and stimulating new ideas that can be tested out later. Descriptive studies emphasize accuracy, precision, and generalizable data. Explanatory studies also value accuracy, precision, and generalizability, but go beyond merely attempting to describe a population's characteristics; they seek to test out hypotheses. The same study can have more than one of these purposes, and the distinction between these purposes in some studies can be fuzzy.

Research studies can be conducted at one point in time or over a longer period. When they focus on point in time, they are cross-sectional studies. Because they observe things at only one time point, cross-sectional studies are limited in attempting to understand causal processes over time. Longitudinal studies, on the other hand, conduct their observations over an extended period and therefore can describe processes occurring over time. Three types of longitudinal studies are trend studies, cohort studies, and panel studies. *Trend studies* observe changes within the same population over time. *Cohort studies* examine how subpopulations change over time. *Panel studies* are like trend and cohort studies, but instead of gathering data from a new set of people each time, they return to gather data from the same individuals each time.

Not all social work research studies gather data from individuals, however. Some gather data on aggregates of people, such as groups or families. Others gather data on social artifacts, such as journal articles, TV commercials, or newspaper editorials. The things that social work researchers seek to observe, describe, and explain—such as individuals, groups, or social artifacts—are called ***units of analysis***. Researchers and consumers of research need to be aware of the risk inherent in making assertions about individuals when the units of analysis for the research are groups or other aggregations. The ecological fallacy occurs when mistaken assertions about individuals are made based on the characteristics that describe an aggregation. For example, if antiabortion graffiti is more likely to appear in low-income neighborhoods that have many abortion clinics, it would be wrong to assert that low-income individuals are more likely to produce antiabortion graffiti.

REVIEW QUESTIONS

1. Which of the following statements about social work research and practice is true?
   a. Practice is practical; research is academic and impractical.
   b. They follow different problem-solving processes.
   c. Only in practice do you have the flexibility to loop back to earlier phases of the process.
   d. All of the above.
   e. None of the above.

2. The problem statement section near the beginning of a research proposal should:
   a. Cite facts
   b. Spell out specific potential useful implications

c. Address a problem that matches the funding source's priorities
d. All of the above
e. None of the above

3. The literature review section of a research proposal should:
   a. Cite comprehensive details about all previous relevant studies
   b. Cite previous research only, not theories
   c. Indicate how the proposed study will relate to, yet go beyond, the prior studies
   d. All of the above
   e. None of the above

4. A good basis for selecting a social work research topic would be:
   a. Information needed to guide a decision about what services to provide
   b. A lack of awareness of the characteristics and needs of a new target population
   c. Whether social workers are implementing an intervention in the intended fashion
   d. Reasons prospective clients don't use services
   e. All of the above
   f. None of the above

5. What would you recommend to a colleague who asked for your advice about the following research question she was considering for a research proposal: Does alcohol abuse influence work performance?
   a. Consider and/or show why the answer is not a foregone conclusion.
   b. Be more specific about both variables in the research question.
   c. Make sure you can get access to observable data.
   d. All of the above.
   e. None of the above.

6. Suppose you are preparing a research proposal to interview family members of persons living with AIDS. Which of the following statements is *not* true?
   a. It would be fairly easy to underestimate the fiscal costs of the study.
   b. It is reasonable to anticipate that agencies working with the target population would be eager to support and cooperate with your study.
   c. The time constraints of the study easily could turn out to be much worse than anticipated.

d. Ethical concerns could impede the study's feasibility.

e. None of the above; they are all true.

f. All of the above; none is true.

7. Which of the following statements is true about the literature review process during problem formulation?

   a. References to studies appear in guides to the literature (like abstracts) as soon as the study is published in a journal.

   b. The literature review should usually be conducted after the research question has been sharpened and the research design has been developed.

   c. Good places to start a literature review include abstracts, bibliographies, and library subject guides and computerized search services.

   d. All of the above.

   e. None of the above.

8. If you want to find out the exact proportion of social workers working in each of the various fields of practice (mental health, child welfare, and so on), you would undertake:

   a. A descriptive study

   b. An exploratory study

   c. A trend study

   d. An explanatory study

   e. A cohort study

9. If you want to obtain tentative new insights about the emotional impact on parents of caregiving for their child with AIDS, you would undertake:

   a. A descriptive study

   b. An exploratory study

   c. A trend study

   d. An explanatory study

   e. A cohort study

10. If you want to find out whether the intervention you have designed really reduces depression, you would undertake:

   a. A descriptive study

   b. An exploratory study

   c. A trend study

   d. An explanatory study

   e. A cohort study

11. If you evaluate your support group intervention by comparing the average improvement in depression among the individuals participating in your support group to the average improvement among the individuals participating in a different kind of group, your unit of analysis would be:

   a. Groups

   b. Individuals

   c. Social artifacts

   d. Depression

12. After conducting a study that finds that states with liberal social welfare policies and more liberal voters have higher rates of child abuse than states with conservative social welfare policies and more conservative voters, you conclude that liberals are more likely to abuse children than are conservatives. Which of the following statements is true about this example?
    a. It illustrates the ecological fallacy.
    b. It illustrates reductionism.
    c. It illustrates good deductive reasoning.
    d. Individuals were the unit of analysis.
    e. None of the above.

EXERCISE 4.1

Suppose you are administering a federally funded demonstration project aimed at preserving families in which children are at risk for neglect or abuse because one or both parents is abusing alcohol or drugs. Suppose you are required to evaluate the three-year program each year. Suppose that the first-year evaluation finds that instead of having fewer children placed in foster care due to neglect or abuse, the families receiving your services had more children placed in foster care. That is, families that received more home visits from your demonstration program were less likely to be preserved than families receiving much fewer visits from your agency's routine services.

1. Discuss how this finding could loop back to generate a new research process all over again.

2. What would the new research question be?

3. Was the purpose of first study (as indicated above) exploratory, descriptive, or explanatory? Explain. Which of these purposes best applies to your new research question (see the previous question)? Explain.

EXERCISE 4.2

Identify eight basic elements (or sections) that would commonly be addressed in a research proposal.

EXERCISE 4.3

Suppose you administer a very small refugee resettlement agency that struggles each year to procure enough voluntary contributions to survive. Suppose one of your three social workers asks you for release time and some funds to research the following two questions:

1. Is the number of applications for political asylum from countries with large populations larger than the number of such applications from countries with small populations?

2. Is it easier to resettle refugees who had jobs and families in their new country before they arrived than refugees who did not have these?

What criteria regarding topic selection from Chapter 4 would you cite in gently and tactfully denying the staff member's request?

EXERCISE 4.4

Suppose you come up with a research question that strikes you as having great value to your agency and perhaps to social workers in other agencies. Describe the steps you would take to assess thoroughly whether and how to pursue that topic and to formulate your research problem. What issues would you address in this problem formulation process?

EXERCISE 4.5

Suppose you work in a child guidance center where the primary intervention modalities include individual, group, family, and art therapy. Devise a research question, or several questions, illustrating how individuals, groups, and social artifacts could be used as the units of analysis. Explain how each would be used. Be sure that each of the three types of units is illustrated in your answer.

EXERCISE 4.6

Suppose you are interested in studying issues in refugee resettlement. Show how a specific topic in this area would be researched differently for each of the following designs: cross-sectional, trend, cohort, and panel.

EXERCISE 4.7

Suppose you find in one of your studies on refugee resettlement that communities with larger numbers of refugees have higher crime rates. Your research assistant writes a first draft of the research report and concludes that this finding indicates that refugees contribute to a higher crime rate. How would you explain the ecological fallacy the assistant is making?

DISCUSSION QUESTIONS

1. Discuss the steps you would take and the sources you would examine to ensure that your literature review would be thorough.

2. Suppose a social work doctoral student concerned with feminist issues wanted to undertake a doctoral dissertation focusing on the following research question: What role does earlier sexual abuse in their lives play in influencing women's decisions to become topless dancers? Discuss why you think this research question does or does not fall within the boundaries of *social work* research. If you think it does not fall within social work boundaries, discuss how the graduate student could modify the question to fit more clearly within social work boundaries.

3. Some people argue that explanatory studies are more important than exploratory or descriptive studies. Do you agree? Why or why not?

CHAPTER

Conceptualization and Operationalization

OBJECTIVES

1. Define independent, dependent, and extraneous variables.
2. Provide an example of a hypothesis and identify its independent variable and dependent variable.
3. Illustrate how an extraneous variable, when controlled, might explain away a relationship between an independent and dependent variable.
4. Illustrate how the same variable can be independent, dependent, or extraneous, depending on the nature and conceptualization of the study.
5. Provide examples of positive, negative, and curvilinear relationships.
6. Discuss how operational definitions differ from other types of definitions.
7. Provide three examples of abstract social work constructs and how each could be operationally defined.
8. Using the same examples as in objective 7, or using other examples, illustrate the variety of reasonable alternative choices available to operationally define the same variable.
9. Explain why some researchers believe that we can measure anything that exists, and illustrate how in attempting to measure things that exist, they often measure things that don't really exist in the real world.
10. Define and illustrate reification.
11. Discuss the role of existing scales in operationally defining variables, including their advantages and disadvantages.
12. Identify four issues to be considered in choosing the most appropriate existing scale as an operational definition for a particular variable in a particular study.

PRACTICE-RELEVANT SUMMARY

If you've had experience in social work practice settings, you probably have observed that the terms emphasized in this chapter—terms like *operational definitions, extraneous variables,* and so forth—are not commonly used by social work practitioners. And yet those terms are highly applicable to the daily practices of social workers.

Consider, for example, the material on conceptual explication discussed at the beginning of the chapter. In the assessment phase of direct practice, we deal with presenting problems that we investigate clinically. We seek to understand why a particular target problem is occurring. What is causing it? What seems to have been helpful to the client system in the past in dealing with the problem? These questions imply hypotheses, which consist of independent and dependent variables. The postulated, tentative explanation is the *hypothesis.* What we think may explain variation in the target problem is the *independent variable;* the variation in the target problem that we seek to explain is the *dependent variable.*

We even deal with *extraneous variables.* Suppose we are treating a child who has been chronically depressed, and we note that each time his depressive symptoms worsen we provide a brief cognitive-behavioral intervention for several sessions and then the symptoms ameliorate. Suppose we are discussing our independent variable (the nature of our intervention) and dependent variable (degree of depressive symptomatology) with other members of the clinical team, and a colleague notes that the symptoms seem to worsen shortly before school resumes after extended summer and Christmas vacations and then ameliorate after a couple of weeks of classes. In wondering whether the resumption of school is the real cause of the swings in depressive symptomatology, our colleague is postulating this as an extraneous variable. Another colleague might postulate the taking of antidepressant medication as another extraneous variable, noting that the child begins taking the medication at the same times that our intervention takes place and then stops taking it after things get better.

Note that there is nothing inherent in any of these variables that makes them independent, dependent, or extraneous. We can postulate that the closer to school resuming (the independent variable), the more the depressive symptoms (the dependent variable). This would be a positive relationship, because both variables increase together. We can postulate the more consistently the client takes antidepressants (the independent variable), the less the depressive symptoms (the dependent variable). This would be a negative (or inverse) relationship, because as one variable increases the other decreases.

Note also that operational definitions are implicit in this illustration. How would the practitioner, her colleagues, or the client know that depressive symptoms are ameliorating or worsening unless they were able to speak in observable terms about the indicators of depression? Social work practitioners, like social work researchers, have a wide variety of options available for operationally defining concepts. In the above illustration, for example, they might observe the client's mood during the interview. They might rely on parent reports of how often the client cries, stays secluded in his room, and so on. They might rely on client self-reports of similar behaviors. Alternatively, they might administer a paper-and-pencil depression scale to the client. Or they might even do all of these.

Perhaps the trickiest idea in this chapter is the notion that we can measure concepts like depression on the one hand, yet on the other hand we can point out that abstract concepts like depression don't really exist in the real world. The term *depression* is nothing more than a mental image—a summary device for bringing together observations and experiences that have something in common. Because depression is just a summary word, we cannot measure it directly. But by operationally defining it we can specify the observable components it covers (that is, crying, remaining isolated, and so on) and then directly measure those indicators. In so doing, we indirectly measure the concept of depression.

Many purely qualitative studies do not articulate operational definitions. Rather than restrict their observations to predetermined operational indicators, researchers conducting qualitative studies often prefer to let the meanings of phenomena emerge from their observations.

REVIEW QUESTIONS

1. Which of the following is *not* an attribute of a good hypothesis?
   a. It should be clear and specific.
   b. It should be a truism.
   c. It should be value-free.
   d. It should be testable.

2. If we test the hypothesis that the well-being of abused children will be better after they are placed with relatives than after they are placed in foster care not with relatives, and we find that this is true only for children above a certain age, then age is what kind of variable?
   a. Independent
   b. Dependent
   c. Control or extraneous
   d. Independent or dependent, depending on whether it is stated at the beginning or end of the hypothesis

3. In the example in question 2 above, level of well-being is what kind of variable?
   a. Independent
   b. Dependent
   c. Control or extraneous
   d. Independent or dependent, depending on whether it is stated at the beginning or end of the hypothesis

4. In the example in question 2 above, where placed (that is, type of placement) is what kind of variable?
   a. Independent

b. Dependent

c. Control or extraneous

d. Independent or dependent, depending on whether it is stated at the beginning or end of the hypothesis

5. In social work studies testing hypotheses involving the variable "marital satisfaction," that variable is:

   a. Always the independent variable

   b. Always the dependent variable

   c. Either independent or dependent, depending on how it is being conceptualized in a particular study

   d. Independent or dependent, depending on whether it is stated at the beginning or end of the hypothesis

   e. Both c and d are true

6. If children who have been in foster care longer also have more behavioral problems, then this is what kind of relationship?

   a. Positive

   b. Negative

   c. Curvilinear

   d. Causal

7. If children who have been in foster care longer have fewer behavioral problems, then this is what kind of relationship?

   a. Positive

   b. Negative

   c. Curvilinear

   d. Causal

8. Suppose children who witness more marital violence express more anxiety than those who witness less violence, but that after a certain extremely high level of violence witnessed they become numb and then express less anxiety than those witnessing moderate levels of violence. This is what kind of relationship?

   a. Positive

   b. Negative

   c. Curvilinear

   d. None of the above

9. Which of the following would *not* be part of an operational definition of children's well-being?

   a. Degree of unhappiness

   b. Score on a child behavior problem scale

   c. Whether or not in residential care for emotional disorder

   d. School performance records, indicating grades, truancy, or tardiness, for example

10. Which of the following statements is true about the text's argument about measuring anything that exists and about reification?
    a. We can directly measure anything that exists.
    b. We can indirectly measure some abstract concepts that don't exist.
    c. It is incorrect to assume that some concepts exist in the real world just because we can measure their indicators.
    d. All of the above.

11. Which of the following statements is true about choosing an existing scale to administer to children as an operational definition of their level of depression before and after treatment?
    a. It should be lengthy; brief scales are too risky.
    b. It should not show changes in scores over time unless the degree of improvement has been substantial.
    c. It should be easy for the children to complete.
    d. It should be reliable and valid.
    e. All of the above are true.
    f. Only c and d are true.

EXERCISE 5.1

Select one of the following concepts: level of caregiver burden, quality of life, feminism, culturally sensitive practice.

1. Provide a conceptual, or theoretical, definition of the concept.

2. Specify two different, reasonable ways to operationally define the concept.

EXERCISE 5.2

Consider the following three variables: level of client functioning, quality of worker-client relationship, number of services utilized.

1. Specify a hypothesis involving two of these variables, and explain how the third might operate as an extraneous variable and what could be done to control for it.

2. Specify another hypothesis involving the above variables, but change the independent and dependent variables. Explain how this could be.

EXERCISE 5.3

Consider the variables: (1) duration of caregiving for an elderly parent with Alzheimer's disease, and (2) degree of caregiver burden. Draw a graph depicting a curvilinear relationship between these variables and explain how this could be.

DISCUSSION QUESTIONS

1. Not everyone agrees with the assertion in the textbook that we can measure anything that exists. Some argue that social work practitioners commonly know and deal with things about their clients that they cannot measure. Do you agree? Why or why not?

2. Using either the concept of feminism or level of caregiver burden, explain what it would mean to reify the concept. Explain how we can measure the concept on the one hand, yet claim it doesn't exist on the other.

CHAPTER

Measurement

OBJECTIVES

1. Explain the difference between nominal and other levels of measurement and give an example of a variable at the nominal level of measurement.
2. Explain the difference between ordinal and higher levels of measurement (that is, interval or ratio) and give an example of a variable at the ordinal level of measurement.
3. Identify the criteria for ratio-level measurement and give an example of a variable at that level.
4. Explain how variables at higher levels of measurement can be collapsed to lower levels and provide an example of this process.
5. Define and give an example of random measurement error.
6. Define and give an example of systematic measurement error.
7. Identify two common biases that contribute to systematic measurement error and explain how they operate.
8. Explain the purpose of triangulation and give an example of it.
9. Define reliability.
10. Identify three types of reliability and explain how each could be assessed.
11. Define validity.
12. Identify and define three types of validity.
13. Explain the difference between criterion and construct validity and give an example of each.
14. Discuss the relationship between reliability and validity.
15. Discuss how reliability and validity are approached in qualitative research in a different manner than in quantitative research.

PRACTICE-RELEVANT SUMMARY

Although social work practitioners and researchers may use different language when they deal with measurement, and although the term *measurement* may be more commonly employed when research is being discussed than during practitioners' daily discourse, measurement is an integral part of social work practice. When practitioners interview clients for the purpose of treatment planning, for example, they are measuring things. They may be measuring the nature and severity of the target problem. They may be measuring other problems and forces that influence the target problem. They may be estimating the extent of motivation, capacity, and opportunity in the client system to alleviate the target problem. They may note that different parts of the client system provide conflicting information, and they may therefore have to make measurement decisions about how to handle these inconsistent measures.

Although practitioners may use different language than researchers when they notice these measurement problems, they are dealing with essentially the same principles as are discussed in this chapter. For example, if they notice that a person contradicts something he or she said earlier, they will realize that something is amiss in the information being provided, because the information is inconsistent. When people provide inconsistent information, researchers call the information unreliable. The term *reliability* refers to the degree of consistency in the information.

Researchers and practitioners can encounter three major forms of consistency (or inconsistency), or reliability (or unreliability), in their information. One form occurs when informants provide information at one point in time that is consistent (or inconsistent) with information they provided at an earlier point in time. This is called *test-retest reliability.* One problem with this form of reliability is that sometimes the reality being depicted by informants really does change between the two time points at which information is provided. However, researchers may still need to assess this form of reliability, particularly if they are assessing the stability of a measure over time.

Another form of reliability is assessed in connection to whether different pieces of information given at the same point in time, by the same informant, are consistent. This is called *internal consistency reliability.* If a divorced mother tells you, early in an interview, that she wants to keep custody of her son, but later in the interview indicates that perhaps it would be best if he lived with his father, you may note a potential inconsistency between the two statements uttered during the same interview. You would be concerned with the internal consistency reliability of the information. Researchers would be worrying about the same type of reliability if they noted contradictory responses to similar items of the same measurement scale.

A third form of reliability deals with whether different people are consistent in the information they provide. Thus, if a mother portrays a child as well behaved, but the father portrays the child as defiant and disobedient, a practitioner would see inconsistency. Researchers term this form of reliability *interrater reliability.* Researchers are typically concerned with this form of reliability when they are using experts to rate something, such as the quality of an interview or the severity of an emotional problem.

Regardless of which type of reliability we use, the implication of inconsistency is the same: if the information is inconsistent, something is wrong with some part of it. Researchers term this form of measurement error *random error,* because there is nothing occurring in a systematic fashion to consistently produce the same misleading information. Random error commonly occurs when respondents don't understand our questions, are fatigued, or aren't concentrating on what is being said.

Practitioners as well as researchers also recognize that information can be consistent but still be wrong. Thus, the child welfare worker investigating reported child abuse realizes that just because a respondent consistently denies abuse, that doesn't guarantee that the truth is being told. Fear of the consequences of affirming the abuse may lead to a bias that consistently results in erroneous information. Researchers call this type of error (or bias) *systematic error.*

When researchers refer to the degree to which a measurement approach avoids systematic error, they refer to the *validity* of the measure. Measures can be reliable, but not valid. Reliability is a necessary, but not sufficient condition for validity. The two most important types of validity a measure may have are *criterion-related validity* and *construct validity. Criterion-related validity* is assessed by seeing if the measure in question produces information correlated by an independent, external measure of the same construct. Thus, a scale to measure posttraumatic stress disorder (PTSD) would have criterion-relation validity if people undergoing treatment for PTSD score worse on it than people who are not in treatment for PTSD.

Construct validity is assessed by seeing if the measure in question produces data more consistent with an independent criterion of the same construct than with a criterion of a related construct. Thus, the above PTSD scale would have criterion-related validity but not construct validity, if the difference in scores on it between people undergoing treatment for depression and those not in treatment for depression was greater than the difference between the PTSD criterion groups. In addition to the above form of validity, you may also encounter the terms *face validity* and *content validity. Face validity* refers primarily to whether items in the measure merely appear to be valid indicators of the concept intended to be measured. *Content validity* refers to whether expert judges agree that the measure covers the full range of meanings included within the concept.

Qualitative researchers approach issues of reliability and validity somewhat differently than quantitative researchers. Qualitative inquiry relies less on standardized instruments. Instead, validity is pursued through in-depth observations and interviews with much smaller samples. The idea is not to come up with a particular measure that can be utilized repeatedly in a standardized fashion to quickly measure the same concept across large numbers of people. Instead, the idea is to describe the everyday lives and deep personal meanings of people in such rich detail that readers would understand what was measured and what it meant without having to wonder if a particular instrument has validity or reliability. Qualitative researchers who follow different epistemological paradigms disagree on the nature and extent of the role of assessing the reliability and validity of their work.

So far, this summary has dealt with the most practice-relevant aspects of Chapter 6. As a result, the first part of the chapter was skipped. Researchers are much more likely than practitioners to be concerned with that part, which pertains to levels of measurement. Researchers need to take into account whether they are going to measure qualitative categories (gender, ethnicity, and so on) or quantitative aspects of a variable (how much of something). Measures using only qualitative categories are at the *nominal* level of measurement. Quantitative measures in social work are usually either at the ordinal or ratio level. *Ordinal* measures only can tell whether something has more or less of something than another thing; they cannot provide information on precisely how much more or less that is. Thus, a measure telling you that some clients were very satisfied with services, while others were moderately satisfied, is an ordinal measure. A *ratio* measure can provide precise differences, and its information can be used arithmetically because it employs an absolute zero point. Thus, a measure that tells you how many days a child has been in foster care is a ratio measure.

REVIEW QUESTIONS

1. An instrument that assesses emotional disorder is at what level of measurement?
   a. Nominal
   b. Ordinal
   c. Ratio
   d. Not enough information to know

2. A measure that indicates exactly how many times in the last week a child saw his parent become inebriated would be at what measurement level?
   a. Nominal
   b. Ordinal
   c. Ratio
   d. Not enough information to know

3. What level of measurement would you have if you asked a child whether his parent became inebriated very often, often, sometimes, rarely, or never?
   a. Nominal
   b. Ordinal
   c. Ratio
   d. Not enough information to know

4. What level of measurement would you have if you asked a child whether the single parent he lives with is his mother or father?
   a. Nominal
   b. Ordinal
   c. Ratio
   d. Interval

5. Suppose you have a brother and a sister complete a complicated scale to assess the extent of alcohol abuse among their parents. Suppose one's answers indicate a lot of abuse, while the other's indicated very little abuse. This would be an example of:
   a. Potential systematic measurement error
   b. Possible unreliability
   c. Possible bias
   d. All of the above

6. The child who denied his parents' truly high level of alcohol abuse (in question 5 above) might be responding in a manner that can be called:
   a. Social desirability bias
   b. Acquiescent response set
   c. Random error
   d. Triangulation

7. If the child responding to the above scale did not understand the complex language in it, his answers would likely contain:
   a. Social desirability bias
   b. Acquiescent response set
   c. Random error
   d. Triangulation
   e. Systematic error

8. In the above scale you find that responses to some items contradict responses to other items. This is an example of:
   a. Poor face validity
   b. Low internal consistency reliability
   c. Low test-retest reliability
   d. Low interrater reliability

9. When we administer the same scale twice to the same people, we are seeking to assess the scale's:
   a. Face validity
   b. Construct validity
   c. Internal consistency reliability
   d. Test-retest reliability
   e. Criterion-related validity

10. You show your scale to your distinguished professor, an internationally renowned expert on the problem being measured, and she enthusiastically agrees that every item on the scale looks excellent.
    a. This supports the scale's face validity.
    b. This does not support the scale's empirical validity.
    c. More testing of the scale's validity is needed.
    d. You can be confident that the scale has criterion-related or construct validity.
    e. All of the above.
    f. a, b, and c are true.

11. You find that people in treatment for low self-esteem have an average score of 20 on your self-esteem scale, indicating much lower self-esteem than people not in treatment, whose average score is 40. Then you administer your self-esteem scale to people in treatment and not in treatment for depression. The average score is 10 for those in treatment for depression and 50 for those not in treatment. You have shown that your scale:
    a. Has criterion-related validity
    b. Lacks construct validity

c. May be measuring depression more than self-esteem

d. All of the above

12. Which of the following statements is/are true about how reliability and validity are approached in qualitative studies?

    a. Qualitative inquiry relies less on standardized instruments.

    b. In qualitative inquiry validity is pursued through in-depth observations and interviews.

    c. In qualitative inquiry the idea is to describe the everyday lives and deep personal meanings of people in rich detail.

    d. Qualitative researchers who follow different epistemological paradigms disagree about the role of assessing the reliability and validity of their work.

    e. All of the above.

EXERCISE 6.1

Suppose you wanted to see whether your special family preservation demonstration project is a more successful/effective way to intervene with families referred for child abuse or neglect than is your agency's routine program of services. You decide to compare the outcome of the two programs on the following three indicators:

a. Type of permanent placement at end of treatment (that is, foster care, institutional, biological parents, and so on)

b. Whether the quality of parenting is rated as excellent, good, fair, or poor

c. Number of days siblings are placed apart from each other

1. Which of the above indicators is at the nominal level of measurement? Explain.

2. Which is at the ordinal level? Explain.

3. Which is at the ratio level? Explain.

EXERCISE 6.2

Suppose you conceptualize a measure to assess whether a client's problem can be considered acute or chronic and, if chronic, the degree of chronicity. Suppose your measure is simply the number of times the client has been previously placed in some form of institutional care for the problem. Show three different ways to report (or categorize) that number. Each way should be at a different level of measurement.

1. Ratio

2. Ordinal

3. Nominal

EXERCISE 6.3

In evaluating the outcome of your family preservation program, you decide to administer lengthy scales to parents, children, and their practitioners in your program and in a comparison program. The scales are designed to assess the well-being of children and the quality of parenting.

1. What are some reasons you might expect to find problems of reliability in the scales?

2. Identify three ways you might assess three different types of reliability regarding the scales.

3. Explain why you would be concerned about the validity of the scales even if you found them reliable. Explain, also, why you might not bother to assess their validity if you found them to be very unreliable.

4. What are some reasons you might expect to find problems of validity in the scales?

5. Identify how you might assess the criterion-related validity of the scales.

EXERCISE 6.4

You are providing a psychoeducational support group intervention to family members caring for a person living with AIDS. You want to measure the degree of stigma the caregivers are experiencing and whether it diminishes after they participate in your group. You can find no suitable measure of stigma, so you design one yourself, consisting of the following four items:

How often do you feel:

Isolated?	________	Often	________	Rarely	________	Never
Ashamed?	________	Often	________	Rarely	________	Never
Hopeless?	________	Often	________	Rarely	________	Never
Like crying?	________	Often	________	Rarely	________	Never

1. What level of measurement do you have?

2. Suppose you assessed the criterion-related validity of your scale and found that individuals entering your group answered “often” much more frequently than individuals who were not caregivers of persons living with AIDS. Suppose, however, that your colleague constructively advised you that although you demonstrated criterion-related validity, that was not enough. In this case, she argued, you need to proceed to assess construct validity.

a. Explain why she may have reached this conclusion. (What is it about your scale and competing constructs that may have led her to suggest this? Can you think of a competing construct she may have in mind?)

b. Following her advice, how would you go about assessing the scale’s construct validity?

DISCUSSION QUESTIONS

1. Some clinical social workers believe that existing scales that measure clinical problems (self-esteem, depression, parent-child relationships, and so on) should be used routinely during the assessment and later phases of clinical practice. Some others disagree, relying instead on clinical interviews. What do you think about this?

2. Some social workers are drawn to a field of practice in part because of their own life experiences and previous issues that resemble the problems they encounter in that field. But not all social workers in a particular agency are the same in this respect. They have different life experiences and different issues, and they may be attracted to the type of services provided by their agency for different reasons. Suppose you are working in a child and family service agency where caseloads are heavy and assessments are based exclusively on interviews. You are struck by the frequency with which some (but not all) practitioners attribute a child's or a family's difficulties almost exclusively to the father's or the mother's need to be controlling. What are some sources of systematic and random error in this agency's approach to assessment? How could the agency assess the reliability and validity of its assessment practices?

3. Discuss the similarities and differences between qualitative and quantitative inquiry with regard to how issues of reliability and validity are handled.

CHAPTER

Constructing Measurement Instruments

OBJECTIVES

1. Construct items for a questionnaire that include both closed- and open-ended questions.
2. Show how the same variable can be measured with an open- or closed-ended questions.
3. Identify the reasons why it might be better to choose open- or closed-ended questions, and what the trade-offs are in the choice.
4. Develop a questionnaire that is clear and simple to complete and that avoids questions that are double-barreled, overly difficult or complex, irrelevant, biased, or illogically sequenced.
5. Recognize flaws in questionnaires developed by others.
6. Identify alternative questionnaire formats.
7. Write clear instructions for a questionnaire and its different sections.
8. Explain the difference between a questionnaire and a scale.
9. Identify the steps taken in identifying potential items for a scale and the criteria used in deciding which ones to include.
10. Construct a brief, simple scale of a variable.
11. Identify different prominent scaling procedures.
12. Identify ways measurement instruments can be culturally insensitive or culturally biased.
13. Identify procedures for anticipating and preventing cultural bias or cultural insensitivity in scale construction.
14. Discuss the similarities and differences between the construction of quantitative and qualitative measurement instruments.

PRACTICE-RELEVANT SUMMARY

Social workers in various roles and fields of practice early in their careers commonly encounter situations where they must construct measurement instruments. Two common situations in which they must construct measurement instruments are when they need to assess client satisfaction with agency services, and when they have to determine client needs for various services. Typically, they will want or be required to construct instruments that are sound from the standpoint of research methodology, even though their purpose may not be to conduct research in the strictest sense. These, however, are not the only examples.

As practitioners begin the process of instrument construction, an early decision may be whether to ask close- or open-ended questions. Open-ended questions are often simpler to construct, and they give respondents the opportunity to answer in their own words and in the way that is most meaningful for them. The downside of this openness, however, is that you may be overwhelmed by the prospect of attempting to process and analyze the vast range of answers you may get to open-ended questions. Moreover, many of the answers may seem irrelevant or hard to decipher. Closed-ended questions, on the other hand, force respondents to answer according to categories that make sense in terms of your research goals, and they are much easier to process. However, they may miss information that clients could supply if an open-ended format were used. When you use closed-ended questions, make sure that your list of response categories is exhaustive and mutually exclusive.

Regardless of whether open- or closed-ended questions are used, they should be as short as possible. They should ask about things that are relevant to respondents and that respondents are capable of answering. They should be worded clearly, in language that respondents understand. Items should not be worded in negative terms. Biasing words or phrases should always be avoided. Also to be avoided are double-barreled questions. These are questions that, sometimes subtly, combine two questions into one, thus leaving the respondent confused about how to answer and the practitioner unsure of what the answer really means.

Questionnaires, or other instruments, should be easy on the eyes and easy to complete. Items should be logically organized. Pages should be uncluttered. It should be clear to respondents where to place their check marks, X's, or other types of response. One option that may simplify responding is the use of contingency questions. These questions are used when some subsequent questions can be answered or skipped depending on how the respondent answers the contingency question. Another simplifying option is to present a matrix format to handle a series of consecutive questions that have the same set of response categories.

It is important to make sure that items are sequenced appropriately. Begin the instrument with items that are easy to answer and interesting. Save the tougher items, or more sensitive ones, for later. Be sensitive to whether and how the answer to one question conceivably might influence an answer to a later question. It is essential that your instrument begin with a clear set of instructions, and that additional instructions appear at the start of each new and different section of the instrument.

Sometimes the instruments you construct will include composite measures in which multiple items are combined to form a quantitative scale. For example, you might include ten items enabling respondents to indicate, on a scale of one to five, how satisfied they are with ten different aspects of service delivery. Then you could sum each client's responses to get an overall satisfaction score for that client. The items you select for your scale should have face validity (as discussed in Chapter 6).

Each should represent one important, and different, aspect of the concept you are attempting to measure. In testing out your items, the responses to each item should vary. If everyone, or almost everyone, answers an item the same way, it offers nothing and should be dropped from the scale. Although not everyone should answer a particular item in the same way, the way people answer each item should be related to how they answer other items. This refers to the internal consistency of the scale (as discussed in Chapter 6). Items that do not relate to other items, or that are overly redundant with other items, should be dropped from the scale. Some prominent scaling procedures that you may want to follow in constructing your scale include Likert scaling and semantic differential scales.

In any field, but perhaps especially in social work, it is essential that your instrument be culturally sensitive. Steps you can take toward having a culturally sensitive instrument include immersion in the culture of the population to be studied before administering a measure developed on other populations, interviewing knowledgeable informants in the study population about the applicability of the measure, the use of bilingual interviewers, translating and back-translating the measure, and pretesting.

If you are conducting a qualitative study, your measurement instruments are likely to differ from instruments used in quantitative studies in several key respects. Qualitative instruments are likely to be much less structured, to rely much more heavily on open-ended questions with in-depth probes, and to be administered in an interview format.

REVIEW QUESTIONS

1. When the variable "ethnicity" of parents is classified as White, African American, or Hispanic, the response categories can be called:

   a. Mutually exclusive
   b. Exhaustive
   c. Both of the above
   d. None of the above

2. The questionnaire item "How satisfied were you and your child with our multifamily and play therapy groups?", with response categories on a four-point scale from very satisfied to very dissatisfied, is an example of:

   a. A double-barreled question
   b. An open-ended question
   c. A negative item
   d. A semantic-differential scale

3. A potential shortcoming of closed-ended questions is:

   a. No opportunity to probe for more information
   b. Some important responses may be omitted from the response categories
   c. Some response categories might not be mutually exclusive
   d. All of the above
   e. None of the above

4. A questionnaire item lists possible social service facilities and asks community residents to enter a check mark beside each one they would *not* want to have located in their community. This is an example of:
   a. A double-barreled question
   b. An open-ended question
   c. A negative item
   d. All of the above

5. Which of the following statements is true about the way you should order items in a self-administered questionnaire?
   a. The order should usually be randomized.
   b. Get the dull items out of the way early; save the interesting ones for later.
   c. Pretesting the questionnaire in different forms can help indicate the best way to order the items.
   d. As long as each item is well constructed, the ordering of items is a minor issue.

6. Which of the following statements is a good guideline for the construction of self-administered questionnaires?
   a. Squeeze as many items as possible on each page to reduce the number of pages.
   b. Provide an introductory statement for each subsection.
   c. Avoid contingency questions; they are too confusing.
   d. All of the above.
   e. None of the above.

7. A Likert scale is developed with half of the items representing positive attitudes about welfare and the other half representing negative attitudes about welfare. Respondent 1 checks "strongly agree" to every item. Respondent 2 checks "strongly disagree" with every item. Respondent 3 checks "agree" with all the positive items and "disagree" with all the negative items. Which of the following statements is true about this example?
   a. Respondent 3 has mixed feelings.
   b. Respondent 1 has the most positive attitude score.
   c. Respondent 3 has the most positive attitude score.
   d. Respondent 2 has the most negative attitude score.
   e. Respondents 1 and 2 have the same attitude score.
   f. Only b and d, are true.
   g. Only c and e are true.

8. Which of the following statements is true about the handling of missing data on some items of a scale?
   a. One acceptable option is to exclude from the analysis those few cases with missing data.
   b. It is sometimes acceptable to assign the middle value to cases with missing data.
   c. It might be acceptable to assign the mean (average) value to the missing item.
   d. All of the above.
   e. None of the above.

9. If you are conducting a qualitative study, your measurement instruments are likely to differ from instruments used in quantitative studies in which of the following respects?
   a. Qualitative instruments are likely to be much less structured.
   b. Qualitative instruments are likely to rely much more heavily on close-ended questions.
   c. Qualitative instruments are less likely to be administered in an interview format.
   d. All of the above.
   e. None of the above.

EXERCISE 7.1

Develop two versions of a brief questionnaire asking other social work students about their experiences in the social work education program. (For example, is it what they expected? Are they learning what they want? What do they want to do when they graduate? And so on.) Make one version entirely open-ended and the other entirely closed-ended. Administer each to a small group of students (perhaps 10 to 20 of them). Compare the answers you get to the two versions. Identify how the sets of answers differed. What advantages and disadvantages of each approach were illustrated by those answers?

EXERCISE 7.2

Suppose a questionnaire is developed to be administered to fourth- through sixth-grade clients in a Child Guidance Center. What is wrong with each of the following items, if they were on such a questionnaire? (Some items may have more than one thing wrong with them.)

1. Do your folks drink? _________ yes _________ no
2. Do you find your parents authoritarian? _________ yes _________ no
3. Do your mother and father work? _________ yes _________ no
4. How many drinks did your father have last week?

_________ yes _________ no

5. Do you cheat in school? _________ yes _________ no
6. What do you want to do when you grow up?

_________ yes _________ no

7. What would you do if you were working on an assignment in class and the student sitting next to you started teasing you and then hit you after you tried to ignore his teasing?

☐ Tell the teacher

☐ Hit the student back

☐ Nothing

8. When your teacher works as hard as he or she can to make school enjoyable, do you think students should be obedient?

_________ yes _________ no

9. Do you agree that your therapist has done his or her job well in the way he or she has worked with you?

_________ yes _________ no

EXERCISE 7.3

Suppose you wanted to construct a scale to assess the quality of services delivered to clients. Discuss how you would identify potential items and select them. On separate pages, develop two versions of a five-item summated scale to assess the above. Use Likert scaling for one and the semantic differential for the other.

EXERCISE 7.4

Suppose you developed the following scale to measure the quality of parent-child relationships and got the following response frequencies in a pilot run of the scale with 100 clients. Which items would you drop from the scale? Why?

1. I love my child
   97 Strongly Agree
   3 Agree
   0 Disagree
   0 Strongly Disagree

2. I hate my child
   0 Strongly Agree
   0 Agree
   2 Disagree
   98 Strongly Disagree

3. I often argue with my child
   20 Strongly Agree
   30 Agree
   30 Disagree
   20 Strongly Disagree

4. My child often embarrasses me
   15 Strongly Agree
   25 Agree
   40 Disagree
   20 Strongly Disagree

DISCUSSION QUESTIONS

1. Discuss the steps you would take to ensure cultural sensitivity in constructing an instrument to assess the degree of burden and needs for social services experienced

by recent Korean immigrants who are family caregivers of relatives with Alzheimer's disease.

2. Discuss what is wrong with the following questionnaire item, how it would be difficult to answer, and the ways responses might be misleading.

In caring for your relative with Alzheimer's disease, do you feel the need for more social support and respite services?

3. Discuss the similarities and differences between the construction of quantitative and qualitative measurement instruments.

CHAPTER

The Logic of Sampling

OBJECTIVES

1. Define sampling and distinguish between the following terms: sample, population, and sampling frame.
2. Provide an example of how social workers commonly use sampling as part of their everyday practice.
3. Provide an example of sampling bias in social work practice.
4. Provide an example of a sampling frame that is biased with regard to a particular target population of concern to social workers.
5. Using a hypothetical example from social work practice, illustrate sampling error resulting from a sample size that is too small.
6. Describe the key feature of probability sampling, and explain how it safeguards against sampling bias.
7. Describe and illustrate the following major types of probability sampling and their functions: simple random sampling; systematic sampling; stratified sampling; and multistage cluster sampling.
8. Utilize tables of estimated sampling error for specific sample sizes, and explain what they mean regarding sampling error and confidence intervals.
9. Identify two reasons why nonprobability sampling techniques are often used in social work research and practice, and provide an example that would require the use of a nonprobability sampling technique.
10. Describe and illustrate the methods, functions, and risks for each of the following types of nonprobability sampling: purposive or judgmental sampling, quota sampling, reliance on available subjects, and snowball sampling.
11. Provide an example of gender bias in sampling.

PRACTICE-RELEVANT SUMMARY

Sampling is the process of selecting observations. In research, the sampling process is selected in a deliberate, strategic manner in which the researcher decides whom or what to observe as a basis for generating new ideas, testing hypotheses, or generalizing about the characteristics of a population. In life outside of the research arena, we all conduct a less systematic, less conscious form of sampling as we make decisions in our daily lives based on incomplete sets of observations. We may, for example, ask our friends about their experiences with their automobiles as one basis for deciding what brand of car to buy. Or we may decide to see a movie that several people recommended. Chances are you decided to enter the field of social work based on an incomplete set of observations (that is, a sample) about this profession. As you amass more observations about social work in your classroom study and fieldwork, you will enlarge your sample and learn whether your original sample gave you a reasonably accurate portrayal of the profession.

Daily sampling decisions also are made in social work practice. Direct-practice decisions about recommended intervention plans, for example, may be made on an incomplete set of observations based on what segments of a client system say or do while in your office. This sample of observations may or may not give an accurate portrayal of how all the members of a client system function away from your office. Decisions about what services to offer may be made based on what is said at a community or agency meeting. The people who attend or are most vocal at that meeting may or may not present an accurate portrayal of the kinds of services that are most needed. Perhaps the people with the greatest needs are the least likely to attend the meeting or the most reticent about speaking up. Decisions about agency processes may be made based on client feedback. But perhaps only the most satisfied clients provide the feedback; perhaps the most dissatisfied ones don't bother, and therefore the feedback is misleadingly positive and fails to identify needed changes. As you gain experience in this (or any other) profession, you will probably encounter a few administrators who favor a form of sampling in which they only seek out the opinions of staff members who always agree with them. These administrators, and their sycophants, are probably unaware of the bias in this form of sampling, believing that they simply provide the best set of observations and that those outside the in-group are outside because they provide less valuable observations.

Daily practice decisions, therefore, can be faulty if they are based on a faulty sample of observations. Samples of observations can be faulty and consequently misleading if the sampling process is biased, as in the examples above. Faulty and misleading decisions can also result from a sample that is too small. It would be foolhardy to bet a large sum on the outcome of an election based only on the candidate your next-door neighbor favors. In social work practice it would be foolhardy to invest a great deal of time and other resources in developing a large new program based on what only a couple of people said they needed.

Scientific sampling procedures have been developed so that we can minimize the likelihood that the samples we select will be biased or too small. These procedures are a critical part of social research. They can also be applied in making practice decisions, and when they cannot be applied, practitioners should at least be mindful of the risks they take when they base decisions on unscientifically selected samples.

The key feature of scientific sampling is the use of *probability methods,* which make it possible for every member of a population to have an equal chance of being selected into the sample. These methods also make it possible to estimate the amount of sampling error that can be expected in a given sample size. *Random selection* is the key to this process. Random selection does not mean haphazard selection; it is a careful, precise process. In *simple random sampling,* for example, each unit of a population is assigned a number. A table of random numbers is used to generate a list of random numbers, and the units having those numbers are included in the sample. An acceptable alternative to simple random sampling, one that may be more practical to use, is *systematic sampling*. A systematic sample is drawn by selecting every *k*th unit in a population.

For even greater precision, and to ensure adequate numbers of small subgroups (ethnic minorities, perhaps) in the sample, *stratified sampling* can be used. With this method, rather than selecting our sample from one overall list of the total population, we begin by breaking that list down into lists of homogeneous subsets of the population. For example, we may break it down into six lists, one list for each of the following ethnic groups: African Americans, Asian Americans, Mexican Americans, Native Americans, Whites, and Others. Then we would randomly or systematically select the appropriate number of elements from each list.

Another sampling technique, *multistage cluster sampling*, is used when the members of a population cannot be easily listed, or when they are geographically so dispersed as to make it too costly to travel great distances to reach small numbers of selected elements. If the elements of the population are already grouped into clusters (churches, schools, and so on), a list of all clusters can be sampled using any of the three foregoing probability sampling techniques. After the clusters are selected in this way, elements within each cluster can be selected using the same techniques.

When we use probability sampling techniques, we can estimate in advance the amount of sampling error likely to occur given specific sample sizes and, knowing this, we can decide how large of a sample to select. Although this process involves statistical formulas that some readers may find overly complex, a fairly simple table can be examined (Table 8-1 in the text, for example) to guide us.

An important caveat in the use of probability sampling involves the distinction between populations and sampling frames. A sampling frame is the list of elements from which a probability sample is selected. Some limited sampling frames fail to include certain segments of the population. Thus, if you selected a probability sample of spouse abusers based on a sampling frame that lists only the spouse abusers receiving treatment for spouse abuse, your probability sample would not be representative of the population of spouse abusers, because those not in treatment would be excluded. If you sought to generalize only to the segment of the population of spouse abusers who are in treatment, your sampling frame would be fine. But using it to generalize to the entire population of spouse abusers would yield a biased sample, despite the use of probability sampling.

Although it is important for you to understand the basics of probability sampling techniques and to utilize them when possible, you also should know that feasibility constraints frequently prevent the use of probability sampling in social work research and practice. Instead, practitioners and researchers often must *rely on their judgment to purposively* select a sample that seems representative or that seems to fit the purpose of the inquiry. Sometimes they simply *rely on available subjects* to whom they have easy and inexpensive access for data gathering. For some inquiries, such as in surveying the homeless or undocumented immigrants, subjects are hard to identify or find. Under these conditions, snowball sampling is used. This involves asking subjects you locate to guide you to other members of the target population, and then asking each additional subject you locate to help you find additional members whom they know. This is called *snowball sampling,* since subjects are accumulated gradually in a snowball fashion.

All of the foregoing sampling techniques that do not involve the use of probability methods—purposive (or judgment) sampling, reliance on available subjects, and snowball sampling—are called *nonprobability sampling procedures.* You probably will have to use these procedures frequently. When you do, it is important to be cautious and mindful of the risks inherent in not using probability techniques. To help offset these risks, sometimes a nonprobability technique called *quota sampling* is used. Using this technique, you select a specified proportion of subjects with specific characteristics (such as gender, ethnicity, and so on). Although using quotas may improve a nonprobability sample, it does not guarantee protection against sampling biases, as does probability sampling.

Sometimes you will encounter studies that make no effort to be representative of or generalize to a population. These studies often will be called *qualitative investigations.* Qualitative studies tend to be more exploratory in nature and seek to probe into deeper meanings among a very small sample. Rather than select samples that are representative, therefore, these studies select theoretically meaningful samples that conceivably may be unrepresentative. Rather than attempt to derive generalizable findings, these studies intend to generate tentative new insights or new hypotheses whose generality can be investigated in future studies. Qualitative studies should not be denigrated because they do not use probability sampling or because they eschew concerns about sampling error or representativeness, since they neither intend nor claim to accurately portray a population. Rather, the quality of the sampling (as well as other methodological features of qualitative studies) should be judged according to whether the study generates tentative new ideas or new ways of looking at things. A qualitative study using nonprobability sampling that gives us a fresh new tentative perspective on a problem, or which helps us understand more deeply its possible meanings to or influences on people, can be just as valuable (if not more so) than a study that uses probability sampling to accurately portray the extent of an already-known phenomenon.

Thus, although probability sampling is less risky than nonprobability sampling from the standpoint of generalizing accurately to a population, some good studies use nonprobability sampling. Rather than think you must always use probability sampling, you should understand when certain sampling techniques are more appropriate than others, the functions of each technique, how feasibility constraints bear on the choice of a sampling procedure, and the risks inherent when samples are too small or vulnerable to bias. Chapter 8 ends with an acknowledgment of one form of sampling bias—gender bias—that has become increasingly evident with the advent of feminism. We should never generalize to both genders when one gender is not adequately represented in the research sample.

REVIEW QUESTIONS

1. Which of the following statements about sampling is *not* true?
   a. It is the process of selecting some elements of a population from a larger set of elements.

b. It makes little difference which sampling method is used; they all provide reasonably accurate information.

c. Large populations, in the millions, can be accurately portrayed with samples of less than 2000.

d. All of the above statements are true.

e. None of the above statements is true.

2. Sampling error can result from:

a. Samples that are too small

b. Biased sampling procedures

c. Biased sampling frames

d. All of the above

3. In general, sampling error decreases as:

a. The sample size increases

b. The population ages

c. The standard deviation increases

d. All of the above

e. None of the above

f. Only a and b are true

4. (Refer to Table 8-1 of the text in answering this question.) Suppose you assume that roughly 50% of a state's residents approve of a new proposition to make undocumented immigrants ineligible to receive welfare benefits, and that roughly 50% disapprove. How large will your sample need to be in order for you to be 95% confident that your survey findings are within plus or minus three percentage points of the real approval/disapproval proportions in the state's population?

a. 400

b. 700

c. 1000

d. 1100

5. Which of the following statements is *not* true about probability sampling?

a. It enables every member of a population to have an equal chance of being selected into the sample.

b. It will always be perfectly representative of the population.

c. It enables us to estimate the degree of sampling error in our data.

d. It is the best way to avoid conscious or unconscious sampling bias.

e. All of the above statements are true.

f. None of the above statements is true.

6. To assess client satisfaction, a social worker in a large family service agency sends a questionnaire to all 1000 clients who completed or dropped out of services during the past two years. Five hundred clients respond to the survey. Which of the following statements is true about this sampling procedure?

a. It was random, since the social worker exerted no influence over who responded and therefore the response pattern was haphazard.

b. The sample was probably representative, since such a large proportion of the population responded.

c. It was not particularly vulnerable to sampling bias.

d. All of the above are true.

e. None of the above is true.

7. A social worker attempts to generate new insights about adult survivors of childhood sexual abuse by conducting in-depth interviews with those survivors she is able to identify and locate. She begins by attending a small self-help group for adult survivors and then asking the members who agree to be interviewed to identify other survivors who might agree to be interviewed. She continues this process with each new interviewee. Which of the following statements is true about this sampling procedure?

   a. It is called snowball sampling.

   b. In light of the circumstances and purpose of the study, it can be more appropriate to use than probability sampling.

   c. It is highly vulnerable to sampling error.

   d. All of the above are true.

   e. None of the above is true.

8. To assess the need in a small and very poor town for parent education classes on child nurturance, a social worker randomly selects telephone numbers from the phone book and then interviews the mother in each home where small children reside. Which of the following statements is/are true about this sampling procedure?

   a. It uses probability sampling techniques.

   b. It involves gender bias.

   c. Its sampling frame might be biased against the very poor.

   d. All of the above.

   e. None of the above.

   f. Only b and c are true.

9. You want to conduct a nationwide study interviewing spouse abusers in spouse abuse treatment programs. You want to minimize sampling error and maximize the representativeness of your sample. You have no population list, but you do have a list of all spouse abuse treatment programs. You have limited travel funds and want to conduct your interviews with as little travel as required for a representative sample. You should:

   a. Conduct cluster sampling

   b. Randomly select a sample of treatment programs, then randomly select participants in the selected programs

c. Conduct simple random sampling
d. Conduct nonprobability sampling
e. None of the above
f. Only a and b
g. Only b and c

10. You want to assess client satisfaction with your large statewide agency's services. You want to make sure that enough members of certain small minority subgroups are included in the sample. You want to minimize sampling error and maximize the representativeness of your sample. You should use:
    a. Cluster sampling
    b. Stratified sampling
    c. Systematic sampling
    d. Quota sampling
    e. Purposive sampling

11. To learn more about spouse abusers in treatment in general you interview every spouse abuser in treatment in your agency. You have interviewed:
    a. The population
    b. A nonprobability quota sample
    c. A nonprobability sample that relied on available subjects
    d. A probability sample
    e. A snowball sample

12. You want to generalize to the nation's population of spouse abusers in treatment. You handpick five treatment programs for your sample because you believe them to be highly representative of the population. You have selected:
    a. A cluster sample
    b. A purposive or judgmental sample
    c. A quota sample
    d. A snowball sample
    e. A simple random sample

Exercises 8.1 to 8.4

On the next page is a made-up list of 100 fictional names of fictional service recipients. Beside each name is the person's fictional ethnicity, their fictional level of satisfaction with services, and whether (in this fictional depiction) they would reply to a mailed questionnaire about their satisfaction with services. This list is to be used in Exercises 8.1 to 8.4.

Name	Ethnicity[1]	Satisfaction[2]	Reply[3]	Name	Ethnicity[1]	Satisfaction[2]	Reply[3]
1. Al Aardvark	W	10	Yes	51. Kara Karson	AfA	5	Yes
2. Ann Average	W	10	Yes	52. Kim Kuang	AsA	5	No
3. Adam Axle	W	10	Yes	53. L. Lau	AsA	5	Yes
4. B. Baker	W	10	Yes	54. L. Lawton	AfA	5	Yes
5. B. Banks	AfA	9	Yes	55. Lynn Lazier	W	5	No
6. B. Bass	W	10	Yes	56. Lara Lemon	AfA	5	Yes
7. C. Canon	NA	9	Yes	57. L. Lennon	W	5	No
8. C. Cielo	H	9	Yes	58. L. Levelle	W	5	Yes
9. C. Chang	AsA	9	Yes	59. L. Loos	AsA	5	Yes
10. C. Connors	W	9	Yes	60. L. Louder	W	5	No
11. C. Culp	W	9	Yes	61. L. Lucky	W	5	No
12. D. Darling	W	9	Yes	62. Mae Mays	AfA	5	No
13. D. Davis	AfA	8	Yes	63. M. Meza	H	5	Yes
14. D. Dierra	H	8	Yes	64. M. Mims	W	5	No
15. Doug Dogma	W	8	Yes	65. M. Minton	W	5	Yes
16. D. Dolman	W	8	Yes	66. M. Mix	AfA	5	No
17. Donny Duck	W	8	Yes	67. M. Mize	W	5	No
18. Ed Eastman	W	8	No	68. M. Moose	W	4	No
19. Eve Eden	W	8	Yes	69. M. Mouse	W	4	No
20. Eva Evans	AfA	8	Yes	70. M. Munson	NA	4	No
21. Emma Evers	W	8	Yes	71. N. Nabisco	W	4	Yes
22. Ezra Ezzio	W	7	Yes	72. N. Neal	AfA	4	Yes
23. Fabio Faber	W	7	Yes	73. N. Nee	AsA	4	No
24. Farah Fay	W	7	Yes	74. N. Nelson	AfA	4	No
25. F. Felman	W	7	Yes	75. N. Nester	W	4	Yes
26. F. Fen	AsA	7	Yes	76. N. Nettles	W	4	Yes
27. F. Fingers	W	7	Yes	77. N. Newton	AfA	4	No
28. F. Fireman	W	7	No	78. N. Noah	W	4	Yes
29. F. Fisher	AfA	7	Yes	79. N. Norman	AfA	4	No
30. G. Gamble	AfA	7	Yes	80. O. Ochs	NA	3	No
31. G. Garcia	H	7	Yes	81. O. Ojeda	H	3	No
32. G. George	NA	7	Yes	82. O. Olson	AfA	3	No
33. F. Gump	W	7	No	83. O. Oltorf	AfA	3	No
34. G. Gutman	W	6	No	84. O. Osmond	AfA	3	Yes
35. Hal Hale	W	6	Yes	85. P. Pan	AsA	3	No
36. Happy Ham	W	6	Yes	86. P. Parker	AfA	3	No
37. H. Hammer	AfA	6	No	87. P. Parks	NA	3	Yes
38. Harry Hank	W	6	Yes	88. P. Parmer	AfA	2	No
39. H. Hidaldo	H	6	Yes	89. R. Raul	H	2	No
40. Helen Hite	W	6	No	90. R. Raupe	H	2	No
41. Kim Ho	AsA	6	Yes	91. R. Reed	AfA	2	Yes
42. Holden Holt	W	6	Yes	92. R. Rhee	AsA	2	No
43. H. Hummer	W	6	No	93. R. Richards	W	2	No
44. Jack Jackson	AfA	6	Yes	94. S. Sue	AsA	2	No
45. Jan Janson	AfA	6	Yes	95. S. Summers	AfA	1	No
46. Jerry Jeep	W	6	No	96. T. Tijerina	H	1	No
47. Jersy Jeffers	W	6	Yes	97. T. Tompkins	W	1	No
48. Jim Jenson	W	6	Yes	98. V. Vazquez	H	1	No
49. Joe Jolson	W	6	No	99. W. Williams	AfA	1	No
50. Jo Joplin	W	6	Yes	100. Z. Zendik	W	1	No

[1]Ethnicity codes: W = White, not Hispanic; AfA = African American; NA = Native American; AsA = Asian American; H = Hispanic.
[2]Level of satisfaction with services from 1 (lowest satisfaction) to 10 (highest satisfaction).
[3]Would they reply to a mailed questionnaire?

Mean level of satisfaction for entire list = 5.48
Number of names in each ethnicity category (the number is the same as the percentage, since the total number is 100) and their mean satisfaction level:

White	50	mean = 6.28
African American	25	mean = 4.64
Hispanic	10	mean = 4.40
Asian American	10	mean = 4.80
Native American	5	mean = 5.20
TOTAL	100	mean = 5.48

Exercises 8.1 to 8.4 involve the use of Appendix D in the text (a table of random numbers) and the box on pages 252–253 of the text, which explains how to use the table of random numbers.

EXERCISE 8.1

1. Select a simple random sample of 20 names from the above list. Briefly explain the procedure you used to select the 20 names.

2. How many members in your sample are from each of the five categories of ethnicity in the above list? How does that compare to their percentages above?

3. Add up the 20 satisfaction scores of the 20 names you randomly selected. Divide the sum by 20 to find the average (mean) satisfaction score of your sample. How close did your sample's mean come to the overall mean of 5.48 from the list? Briefly explain.

4. To what do you attribute the closeness or discrepancies between the proportions of ethnic groups in your sample and the proportions of ethnic groups in the list of 100? To what do you attribute the closeness or discrepancy between the mean satisfaction level of your sample and the overall mean of 5.48 from the list? Briefly explain.

EXERCISE 8.2

1. Repeat Exercise 8.1, but select a systematic sample (beginning with a random start) of 20 names instead of a simple random sample. Briefly explain the procedure you used to select the 20 names.

2. Compare the results with those in Exercise 8.1. Discuss the similarities and differences from the standpoint of sampling error and from the standpoint of whether the two sampling methods are essentially interchangable.

3. Add the mean satisfaction scores of your two samples of 20 names each (the mean from Exercise 8.1 added to the mean of Exercise 8.2). Divide the sum by 2 to obtain a mean of the two means. Does the latter mean come closer to the overall mean of 5.48? Briefly explain why or why not.

EXERCISE 8.3

1. Using the same list of 100 names, select a stratified sample of 20 names, stratifying by ethnicity. Select 10 Whites, 5 African Americans, 2 Hispanics, 2 Asian Americans, and 1 Native American. Briefly explain the procedure you used to select the 20 names.

2. Add up the 20 satisfaction scores of the 20 names in your stratified sample. Divide the sum by 20 to find the average (mean) satisfaction score of your sample. How close did your sample's mean come to the overall mean of 5.48 from the list? How does the accuracy of your stratified sample's mean compare to the accuracy of the means from the simple random sample and from the systematic sample? Is that what you expected? Why or why not? Briefly explain why the stratified sample's mean was or was not closer than the other two means to the overall mean of 5.48.

EXERCISE 8.4

Examine the fourth column of the list of 100 names. Notice that it indicates whether clients would reply to a mailed questionnaire.

1. If your sample consisted only of the names who responded, what type of sample would that be?

2. What would the advantages and disadvantages of that sample be compared to the ones you selected in Exercises 8.1 to 8.3?

3. If you calculate the mean scores of those who would and would not reply, you would find that respondents have a mean satisfaction level of 6.7, whereas the mean for those who would not reply is 3.9. How does the accuracy of the means of the samples you drew in Exercises 8.1 to 8.3 compare to the accuracy of the 6.7 mean of the above fictionalized sample of respondents to a mailed questionnaire? What does this imply for what you would do later on in your professional practice if you ever need to conduct a client satisfaction survey?

EXERCISE 8.5

1. Discuss the conditions under which selecting a purposive sample would be warranted.

2. What would be the risks?

EXERCISE 8.6

1. Discuss the conditions under which selecting a snowball sample would be warranted.

2. What would be the risks?

3. Briefly describe how you would go about selecting a snowball sample of women who have been battered by their mates but have not reported the abuse, have not sought services, and continue to live with the batterer.

DISCUSSION QUESTIONS

1. Your supervisor assigns you to conduct a needs assessment study to ascertain the extent of need in your agency's geographic area for new services not yet provided but that could be developed and offered by your agency. She suggests that you prepare a form asking about need for the new services that current clients can voluntarily fill out and drop in a box while they wait for their appointments. How would you react to her suggestion? Would you suggest an alternative sampling procedure you believe would yield better, more representative information? If so, identify and briefly describe the alternative procedure you would propose. Briefly explain your rationale for agreeing with her suggestion or for proposing the alternative procedure.

2. Although a large number of professional social workers are members of the National Association of Social Workers (NASW), many others are not. Your state chapter of NASW decides to survey social workers in your state to see if they adequately understand legal and ethical codes regarding dual relationships with clients. As an active member of the chapter who has expertise in research methods, you are appointed to chair a committee to conduct the survey. The members of your committee suggest that your sample be randomly selected from the statewide NASW membership list. They argue that because the sample would be random, it would be free from bias. Remembering your research methods text's discussion about the difference between populations and sampling frames, you feel compelled to tactfully point out a potential bias in their suggested procedure, despite the fact that it involves probability sampling. Briefly state your response and specify alternative or additional sampling procedures that you would suggest.

3. You have a limited amount of travel money and time to conduct face-to-face interviews with eighth-graders about their exposure to substance abuse. However, your agency wants your study to be statewide and your sample to be representative of eighth-graders in the state.

a. If you decided to use a probability sampling procedure, which would it be? Briefly describe how you would implement it.

b. If you decided to use a nonprobability sampling procedure that you felt would have the best chance of any nonprobability sampling procedure of yielding a representative sample, which nonprobability sampling procedure would you choose? Briefly describe how you would implement it.

4. Conceptualize and describe a hypothetical example of gender bias in selecting a sample for a social work research study connected to assessing or intervening with a particular problem. Explain how it is biased and the undesirable practical implications of that bias.

CHAPTER

Causal Inference and Group Designs

OBJECTIVES

1. Distinguish when social work practitioners should and should not infer causality, given different logical arrangements under which the information they encounter was obtained.
2. Recognize threats to internal validity that are and are not controlled in the practice evaluation and other research reports social workers commonly encounter in the professional literature or in agency documents.
3. Distinguish between correlation and causality in the practice information social workers encounter.
4. Design a practice evaluation experiment that would permit causal inferences about practice effectiveness.
5. Design a quasi-experimental evaluation of practice that would have sufficient internal validity.
6. Recognize preexperimental designs and their limitations, and know when and how to use them.
7. Describe the potential influence of measurement bias in experimental practice evaluations.
8. Explain the issue of external validity in experimental and quasi-experimental evaluations of practice, and distinguish to whom findings can and cannot be generalized in practice evaluation studies.
9. Describe how nonequivalent control groups and time-series quasi-experimental designs attempt to control for threats to internal validity.
10. Describe three alternative experimental designs and the rationale for using each.
11. Describe the use of waiting lists and alternative, routine services as control conditions, so that clients in control or comparison conditions are not denied services.
12. Discuss the ways that practical pitfalls can impede carrying out experiments and quasi-experiments in social work agencies.
13. Identify qualitative research methods that may be used to help avoid or alleviate the practical pitfalls that can impede carrying out experiments and quasi-experiments in social work agencies.

PRACTICE-RELEVANT SUMMARY

Many social workers, quite early in their careers, find themselves caring quite a bit about a research issue they never anticipated caring about: the design of studies to evaluate practice effectiveness. Often the impetus for their concern is the requirement by funding sources that, in order to obtain funding for a new program or to renew funding for an ongoing program, they must conduct an experiment or quasi-experiment to evaluate the effectiveness of the program for which they seek new or renewed funds. To meet this requirement they commonly will seek out the services of a research methodologist who specializes in the evaluation of programs or interventions. If the social workers never learned, or forgot, the material in Chapter 9, they probably will be puzzled by the research design expectations of the funding source and will have an uncomfortable relationship with their research consultant, who probably will recommend that the evaluation be designed in ways that require that some clients in the study not receive the service being evaluated until after the evaluation is completed.

Many social workers, not well versed in research design, think it should be sufficient merely to measure how well service recipients are doing after receiving the service. These social workers may not recognize that such a *preexperimental* design (a *one-shot case study* is the term for this design) tells us nothing about the degree of change that did or did not occur. Other social workers, also not well versed in research design, think it is enough to show that service recipients are better off after receiving services than before, not recognizing that this *one-group pretest-posttest preexperimental design* fails to take into account myriad other factors that could have been operating during the same period to cause the improvement. The same social workers might also mistakenly believe that simply showing that a group that received services is doing better than any old group that did not happen to receive services is enough to prove that the services are effective. This notion overlooks the very real possibility that the two groups were not comparable to begin with and that perhaps the service recipients were just doing better than the others before services were provided. Because of this shortcoming, this design—the *posttest-only design with nonequivalent groups* (also called the *static-group comparison design*)—is also classified as preexperimental.

Social work practitioners may so strongly believe in the value of the services they provide that they see no need to go beyond preexperimental designs to be convinced that their services are effective. Funding sources, however, are likely to be more skeptical and to require that the services be evaluated with *experimental* or *quasi-experimental* designs. If you propose a preexperimental design for the evaluation, your funder or your research consultant is likely to identify a number of threats to the internal validity of your proposed design. Questioning the design's *internal validity* means questioning whether the design adequately depicts whether the evaluated service is really the cause of the service outcome indicator(s) being measured.

To have a reasonably high degree of internal validity, a design should meet three criteria for inferring causality: (1) the cause (service) should precede the effect (outcome indicator being measured) in time; (2) variation in the provision of service should be empirically correlated with variation in outcome; and (3) alternative explanations for the correlation should be ruled out. Designs that do not meet all three criteria can be criticized for failing to control for certain threats to internal validity. One common threat is history, which refers to other events that may coincide with the services and that may be the real cause of the desired outcome. Another important threat is maturation, or the passage of time. Sometimes clients do better as time passes after a traumatic event, regardless of whether they received services during that period. Likewise, sometimes clients improve as they mature developmentally, regardless of the services they may or may not receive. Often the process of pretesting influences the change that is observed on a posttest. Or perhaps the measures used at posttest were more prone to indicate better functioning than the measures used at pretest. Statistical regression can account for improved posttest scores when subjects are selected for treatment based on their extremely undesirable pretest scores. Selection biases can result in assigning to the evaluated service those cases that have the best chance to improve, or that are functioning better to begin with, and then comparing them to dissimilar cases with worse prognoses or worse preservice functioning. Experimental mortality threatens a study's internal validity when clients not improving drop out of treatment, leaving only those who improved to be tested at posttest. Sometimes the causal time sequence is unclear, such as when service completers are functioning better than premature terminators. Did the better functioning result from completing the service? Or did it explain why some people were better able to complete services than others? Finally, internal validity may be threatened by the diffusion or imitation of treatment, such as when practitioners in other units learn about the "special" service being evaluated and try to imitate it.

The best way to control for threats to internal validity, and thus to have a high degree of internal validity, is by using an experimental design to evaluate your program or intervention. (This is not the same as saying that experimental designs are the best designs for any kind of research. Studies that are not attempting to test causality would not use experimental designs but might produce findings of great value.) The cardinal feature of experimental designs is the use of *random assignment* of clients to an experimental group (service recipients) and to a control group (nonrecipients), to ensure a high mathematical likelihood that the two groups are comparable on all relevant factors except the receipt of the service being evaluated. In social work practice settings, the nonrecipients of the service being tested (that is, those in the control group) need not be denied any type of service. They simply could receive alternative services (usually the agency's routine services), and/or they could be put on a waiting list for the experimental service.

The classical experimental design is the *pretest-posttest control group design*, which compares the two groups according to their improvement from pretest to posttest. A second experimental design, called the *posttest-only control group design*, should be considered when we think that pretest measures might impact treatment effects or bias posttest responses. This design assumes that random assignment ensures pretest equivalence between the two groups, thus permitting the inference that posttest differences reflect the causal impact of the evaluated service. The third experimental design, the *Solomon four-group design*, examines two groups that received pretesting and posttesting and two groups that received posttests only. This design, rare in social work, permits the ferreting out of effects due to testing and effects due to the tested intervention.

Although random assignment to experimental and control groups is a cardinal feature of experimental designs, it alone will not guarantee the control of all threats to internal validity. It does not, for example, prevent experimental mortality. Neither does it prevent measurement bias. No matter how elegant or impressive an experiment may be in other respects, if its measurement procedures appear highly vulnerable to bias favoring the experimental group, the value of the study may be egregiously compromised, and its findings may be highly suspect.

Agency constraints or ethical concerns often may make it impossible to conduct randomized experiments. When this happens, you may be able to use a quasi-experimental design. *Quasi-experimental designs* are better than preexperimental designs because they take some reasonable steps to control for threats to internal validity. Although these steps are not as ideal as random assignment, they can provide sufficient tentative grounds for causal inferences that can guide practice while we await further testing of the services in question.

One commonly useful quasi-experimental design involves the use of a nonequivalent existing control group for which you have data indicating that it appears to be very similar in relevant respects to the experimental group. Both groups are pretested and posttested. Thus, it is like the classical experimental design, except that in lieu of random assignment, data are provided supporting the comparability of the two groups. Another commonly used and valuable set of quasi-experimental designs are called *time-series designs.* The main feature of these designs is the conducting of numerous repeated observations before introducing an intervention and conducting numerous additional repeated observations after introducing the intervention. Conducting numerous observations facilitates our ability to infer whether changes reflect treatment effects as opposed to history, maturation or the passage of time, testing effects, or statistical regression.

No matter how much internal validity your experiment or quasi-experiment may have, that does not guarantee that it will have external validity. *External validity* refers to the extent to which you can generalize the study's findings to settings and individuals beyond the study conditions. The clients participating in a particular study, or the study setting, may be unlike clients and settings elsewhere, and therefore an intervention that worked in the study may not work as well with other clients or in other settings. When you read or report studies it is critical that you pay special heed to the particular characteristics of the study sample and setting and to whom and where the findings can and cannot be generalized. A common problem that may severely limit the generalizability of an experiment or quasi-experiment involves research reactivity. Awareness of participating in a special experiment, or the special measurement procedures utilized in the study, can influence changes that may not occur when the intervention is provided outside of the experimental research context. *Placebo effects* is the term used to refer to changes produced not by the intervention, but by research procedures that make clients feel they are receiving something special. Placebo effects can be controlled by using the *placebo control group design,* which involves randomly assigning clients to an experimental, control, and placebo group.

No matter how rigorous your experimental or quasi-experimental design may be, in social work practice settings you are likely to encounter practical pitfalls in trying to implement your design. These pitfalls may compromise the fidelity of the intervention being evaluated, contaminate the control condition or the case assignment protocol, or hinder client recruitment and retention. Qualitative research methods can be included as part of your quantitative experiment or quasi-experiment to help anticipate, avoid, or alleviate many of the practical pitfalls you are likely to encounter.

Qualitative methods offer a number of ways on-site research staff members can attempt to observe research implementation pitfalls. For example, they can interact formally or informally with agency staff members to identify compliance problems or learn how they are implementing the interventions. They can use videotapes or practitioner activity logs to assess intervention fidelity. They can also identify implementation problems by following along with (shadowing) practitioners in their daily activities. They can participate in in-service trainings or group supervision to identify discrepancies between the intended intervention and what agency trainers or supervisors are proscribing. Additional qualitative methods are described in Chapter 9 and will be examined further in several subsequent chapters.

REVIEW QUESTIONS

1. To evaluate the effectiveness of your case management program aimed at improving school attendance, you compare the changes in school attendance between teens who chose to participate in your program and teens who chose to participate in a program offering a cash incentive for attending school. Attendance increases 50% in your program and 25% in the cash incentive program. You should therefore conclude:

   a. Both programs caused school attendance to increase.
   b. Your case management program caused a greater increase in attendance than did the cash incentive program.
   c. History could account for part of the increase in both programs.
   d. A selection bias could explain the higher increase in your case management program.
   e. Only a and b.
   f. Only c and d.

2. After seeing an adolescent girl and her mother for many family therapy sessions, you realize that the girl's behavior problems are at their worst whenever her mother's moods are at their worst. You should therefore conclude that:

   a. The mother's bad moods are causing the girl's behavior problems.
   b. The girl's behavior problems are causing the mother's bad moods.
   c. The mother's bad moods and the girl's behavior problems are causing each other, in a fashion consistent with social systems theory.
   d. None of the above.

3. An exciting new intervention is developed to alleviate posttraumatic stress symptoms among rape victims. Every practitioner in your rape crisis center tries the new intervention with every new client, and every one of the clients shows remarkable improvement after intervention is completed. You should therefore conclude that:
   a. The intervention has been proven to be effective.
   b. Passage of time, and not the intervention, may have caused the improvement.
   c. History, and not the intervention, may have caused the improvement.
   d. All of the above.
   e. Only b and c.

4. You construct two measures of depression, one to be administered at pretest and one to be administered at posttest. After the pretest, the most depressed clients are assigned to treatment approach A, and the lesser depressed clients are assigned to treatment approach B. After treatment, the approach A clients show significantly more improvement in level of depression than do the approach B clients. You should therefore conclude that:
   a. The results may be due to statistical regression.
   b. The results may be due to instrumentation effects.
   c. Treatment A is more effective.
   d. Only a and b.

5. Which of the following statements is true about the classical, pretest-posttest control group design?
   a. It controls for all threats to internal validity.
   b. It ensures valid measurement.
   c. It ensures unbiased ratings.
   d. All of the above.
   e. None of the above.

6. To evaluate your psychoeducational group treatment approach for dually diagnosed individuals with chronic mental illness and substance abuse problems, you conduct a randomized experiment comparing clients who managed to attend all your program's group sessions to clients randomly assigned to a control group. Since one-third of the clients assigned to your program did not complete it due to flare-ups in their problems during the course of treatment, you eliminated those clients from your posttesting. You find that almost all those who completed your program improved on the outcome measure, whereas in the control group two-thirds improved and one-third worsened. You should therefore conclude that:

a. Your program was effective.

b. Experimental mortality is a plausible explanation for your results.

c. Maturation or the passage of time is a plausible explanation for your results.

d. Only a and b.

7. City officials who fund both a child guidance center and a family service agency decide to conduct a randomized experiment to see which facility is more effective and which, therefore, should receive a funding increase or a funding decrease. The child guidance center traditionally has emphasized play therapy with the child and not provided much family therapy. The family service agency has traditionally emphasized family therapy and not provided much play therapy. Administrators and practitioners in both agencies know about each other's approach and about the purpose of the experiment. The experiment, after randomly assigning clients to each of the two agencies and using valid, unbiased pretests and posttests, ends up finding no difference in outcome between the two agencies. Social workers reading about this study therefore should conclude:

   a. The two agencies seem to have approximately equal effects.

   b. It doesn't seem to matter much whether play therapy or family therapy is emphasized with these clients.

   c. The results may be misleading, due to possible diffusion or imitation of treatments.

   d. Only a and b.

8. Which of the following statements is true about random assignment to experimental and control groups?

   a. It guarantees that the experimental and control groups will be equivalent in the background characteristics of their clients.

   b. With a large enough sample it offers a high mathematical likelihood of avoiding significant inequivalence between the two groups in the background characteristics of their clients.

   c. It involves careful probability sampling procedures in assigning clients to groups.

   d. Haphazard circumstances can determine who gets assigned to which group.

   e. Both b and c, only, are true.

9. A time-series design is used to evaluate whether a county's new family preservation demonstration program, which began in 1990, appears to be reducing out-of-home placements of children. Below are four different chronologically ordered annual out-of-home placement rates for five years before the program began and five years after it began. Which pattern best supports the notion that the program is causing the desired reduction?

						Program Years				
	1986	1987	1988	1989	1990	1991	1992	1993	1994	1995
a.	1000	950	900	850	800	750	700	650	600	550
b.	950	975	960	950	980	750	700	650	600	550
c.	850	980	700	850	800	700	900	850	950	750
d.	700	980	700	950	750	700	900	750	950	700

a. Pattern a best supports the notion that the program is causing the desired reduction.

b. Pattern b best supports the notion that the program is causing the desired reduction.

c. Pattern c best supports the notion that the program is causing the desired reduction.

d. Pattern d best supports the notion that the program is causing the desired reduction.

10. Which of the following statements is true about the nonequivalent control group design?

    a. If evidence of comparibility of groups is provided, it can have a credible degree of internal validity.
    b. It is an experimental design.
    c. It is a preexperimental design.
    d. It has less internal validity than the one-group pretest-posttest design.

11. Which of the following statements is true about the classical experimental design?

    a. Random assignment assures a high likelihood that the study sample is representative of the rest of the target population.
    b. Because of random assignment, the effects observed in the study can be generalized outside of the experimental situation.
    c. In addition to having a high degree of internal validity, it has a high degree of external validity.
    d. All of the above.
    e. None of the above.

12. Which of the following statements is true about implementing experiments and quasi-experiments in service-oriented social work practice agencies?

a. If the study design has high internal validity, we can be fairly certain that practitioners will implement the tested intervention in the intended manner.
b. If the study design has high internal validity, we can be fairly certain that control group members will not be influenced by the tested intervention.
c. If the study design has high internal validity, we can be fairly certain that cases will be assigned to treatment conditions in the intended manner.
d. All of the above.
e. None of the above.

13. What role can qualitative research methods play as part of experimental or quasi-experimental studies?
    a. None; experimental or quasi-experimental studies should be purely quantitative.
    b. They control for threats to internal validity.
    c. They can help us anticipate, avoid, or alleviate practical pitfalls in implementation.
    d. They can help us develop possible explanations for unexpected, puzzling findings.
    e. Both c and d, only, are true.

EXERCISE 9.1

You work in an agency providing crisis intervention services to runaway adolescents and their families. Your administrator suggests that the program's effectiveness be evaluated by pretesting each family immediately after the runaway episode and then posttesting the family after the completion of your services. The pre- and posttests will measure the quality of the relationship between the runaways and their parents. The administrator knows you read an unforgettable textbook on research methods in your research course and therefore asks for your advice on how people with research expertise are likely to respond to the suggested design, particularly with regard to its validity. What would you say regarding the internal validity of the suggested design? Would you recommend using this design? Identify each threat to internal validity and explain why the suggested design does or does not control for it.

EXERCISE 9.2

What would you recommend to control for the threats to internal validity that the design suggested by the administrator in Exercise 9.1 does not control for? Design an experiment to control for those threats. Explain what threats to internal and external validity it does and does not control for.

EXERCISE 9.3

Suppose your administrator (in the foregoing two exercises) was unwilling to support a randomized experimental design but still wanted to conduct an evaluation that would offer scientific credibility as to the effects of the program.

1. Design a nonequivalent control groups quasi-experiment that would be feasible, and explain why you think it would have adequate internal validity.

2. Explain why a time-series design might not be feasible, in light of the fact that your program intervenes immediately during crises.

EXERCISE 9.4

Suppose you work in a state mental health planning agency and want to evaluate the impact of a statewide case management program that began in 1988. The program's aim is to reduce the number of inpatient days spent in state hospitals for mental illness.

1. Design a simple time-series evaluation of the program's impact. Explain why it would be scientifically credible, and identify its limitations from the standpoint of internal validity.

2. Design a multiple time-series evaluation of the program's impact. Explain why it would have more internal validity than a simple time-series evaluation.

EXERCISE 9.5

1. Discuss at least four practical pitfalls often encountered in social work practice settings, and the ways they may adversely influence the carrying out of your experiment or quasi-experiment.

2. Identify qualitative research methods that can be helpful in attempting to anticipate, avoid, or alleviate each of the pitfalls you have identified above.

DISCUSSION QUESTIONS

1. Explain the difference between statistical regression and the passage of time as threats to internal validity. Develop two hypothetical graphs of simple time-series data to illustrate the difference.

2. Explain why random assignment to groups is the ideal way to try to make groups comparable.

3. Discuss why and how an experiment with a high degree of internal validity might not have a high degree of external validity. Include the concepts of representativeness and research reactivity in your answer.

4. As a practitioner seeking to utilize published practice evaluations as a guide to your own practice, would you be less likely to be guided by studies with low internal validity or studies with low external validity? Why?

CHAPTER

Single-Subject Designs

OBJECTIVES

1. Explain the logic of single-subject designs in the evaluation of practice effectiveness.
2. Identify the chief advantages and disadvantages of using single-subject designs instead of group designs to evaluate practice.
3. Discuss the ways that single-subject designs can be used as part of the assessment and monitoring of client problems.
4. Identify practical constraints that can limit the practitioner's ability to conduct rigorous single-case design evaluations.
5. Discuss special problems in measurement and data gathering when practitioners use single-case designs to evaluate their practice.
6. Identify the alternative ways practitioners can gather single-subject design data, and discuss the advantages and disadvantages of each alternative.
7. Explain triangulation and its advantages.
8. Discuss the importance of the baseline phase and identify alternative baseline patterns and their implications.
9. Identify and describe alternative single-subject designs and explain their advantages and disadvantages.
10. Interpret the visual significance and meaning of alternative graphed data patterns in single-subject design results.
11. Discuss the implications of ambiguous data patterns and what to do when they are encountered.
12. Interpret aggregated results of multiple single-subject practice evaluations.
13. Discuss the important role replication can play in the interpretation of single-subject findings.
14. Discuss ethical controversies that apply specifically to practice evaluation using single-subject designs.
15. Be able to employ single-subject designs in your own professional practice.

PRACTICE-RELEVANT SUMMARY

Single-subject designs are time-series designs (discussed in Chapter 9) that can be used to evaluate practice with a single case, such as an individual, a family, or a group. Many social work educators these days believe that single-subject methodology is one of the most relevant research topics for future practitioners, since practitioners can implement these designs themselves, in their own practice, in evaluating their effectiveness with specific cases or in conducting assessment and monitoring.

The key concept in the logic of single-subject designs is the repeated measurement of the target problem many times before and after an intervention begins and seeing whether improvement in the target problem consistently coincides with the onset of the intervention being evaluated.

When you decide to use a single-subject design to evaluate your practice with a particular case, an early challenge involves identifying the appropriate target problem(s) and then operationally defining it. Because any one operational indicator may fail to detect client improvement, the principle of triangulation is commonly employed. *Triangulation* involves the use of two or more indicators or measurement strategies when confronted with a multiplicity of measurement options, all of which have different flaws.

Subsequent decisions must be made about who should conduct the measurement. Should the client self-monitor? Or should someone else do it, such as the practitioner or a client's significant other? Each option has its own unique advantages and disadvantages, and, again, the principle of triangulation can be employed. The same applies to decisions about sources of data, such as available records, interviews, self-report scales, and direct behavioral observations.

If a self-report scale is used, its reliability, validity, and sensitivity to subtle changes become relevant, as does its applicability to frequent repeated measurement in the context of a clinical relationship and setting. Client self-monitoring is very commonly used to measure client progress. This approach is often the most feasible in terms of practitioner resources; moreover, many target problems, such as the frequency of negative thoughts, cannot be measured by anyone other than the client. But self-monitoring is highly vulnerable to client bias and research reactivity. The latter occurs when the process of observing and recording the data influences change in the target problem.

One way to minimize bias and reactivity is through the use of unobtrusive observation, which means observing and recording behavioral data in ways that by and large are not noticable to the people being observed. Unobtrusive observation, however, is very difficult for practitioners to conduct. Data gathered through direct observation can be quantified in terms of frequency, duration, and/or magnitude.

Once you have developed your measurement strategy, the next big challenge involves obtaining an adequate baseline. The baseline is the phase of repeated measures that are gathered before the intervention begins. Baselines are control phases. The graphed pattern of data collected during the baseline phase will be compared to the graphed pattern of data collected during the intervention (experimental) phase. To have a reasonable chance of finding a visually significant improvement in the graphed data pattern after the onset of intervention, the baseline phase ideally should have several attributes. It should involve many measurement points (between five and ten at a minimum). The chronological graphed data pattern should be stable, not fluctuating wildly. Finally, the pattern should not reflect a trend of dramatic improvement to the degree that suggests that the problem is nearing resolution before intervention even begins. (It's great for the client if this happens, of course, but it obviates the utility of the single-subject design and perhaps also the need to apply the intervention to the already dramatically improving target problem.)

When a baseline does not have the above three attributes, it probably should be extended until it does have them. The realities of practice, however, may not let you wait that long. Under these conditions, you simply do the best you can do and hope that the overall data pattern (after the intervention phase is completed) has some utility. In some situations you may even have to obtain a retrospective baseline, which relies on available records or the memory of the client or significant others. When you rely on memory you should use specific, identifiable events that are easy to recall and that go back no more than several weeks.

There are a variety of alternative single-subject designs to choose from. The realities of practice, however, probably will lead you to select the simplest design: the *AB design*. This design includes only one baseline phase (A) and one intervention phase (B). The advantage of this design is its simplicity and the fact that it will often be the only one that practice constraints will permit. However, because it has the potential to detect only one visually significant coincidence in the data pattern (from A to B), it offers less control for history than the alternative designs. Nevertheless, the potential to detect one visually significant shift has enough value to warrant using the AB design when it is the best you can do. Moreover, if the results of an AB design can be consistently replicated in subsequent AB designs involving the same intervention with similar clients and similar target problems, the threat of history becomes farfetched.

The most common alternatives to the AB design build replication into the same study with the same client and thus provide increased control for history within the one study. One alternative is the *ABAB design,* which assumes that if you withdraw the intervention and then reintroduce it you can see if the target problem gets worse (or slows its rate of improvement) during the second baseline (the second A) and then begins to steadily improve again when intervention is reintroduced (during the second B phase). Two major problems with this design are: (1) that practitioners may be unwilling to withdraw an intervention that appears to be working, and (2) improvement on some target problems is irreversible, even when intervention is withdrawn.

Another common alternative is the *multiple-baseline design,* which involves staggering the application of the intervention to different target problems, settings, or individuals. This increases control for history by providing more than one time point at which a dramatic coincidence can occur. Although this design avoids the problems inherent in ABAB designs, it does not get around the possibility that when the intervention is applied to the first target problem or setting its effects may generalize over into other target problems or settings.

Sometimes practitioners will set out to use an AB design, but after finding no improvement during B will try out a different intervention during an added-on (C) phase. If that intervention doesn't appear to be effective, they may then add on a D phase, during which they try a third type of intervention. The results of an ABC or ABCD design should be interpreted with caution. If only the last intervention tried (the C in ABC or the D in ABCD) yields improvement, it is plausible that an extraneous event eventually occurred to cause the improvement or that the last intervention might not have worked had it not been preceded by the previous interventions, which alone were not enough. Replication with subsequent clients, in which the interventions are introduced in varying sequences, will help you sort this out.

In single-subject research, replication enhances both internal and external validity. It enhances internal validity by adding more possibilities to observe consistent unlikely coincidences that help us sort out the plausibility of history (that is, extraneous events) as the cause of changes in the target problem. It enhances external validity by increasing the number and diversity of cases and contexts with which the intervention has been tested.

Single-subject studies also can be enhanced by incorporating qualitative research methods. Qualitative interviews with the client and significant others can help alleviate ambiguity in data patterns by identifying the possible occurence of extraneous events. Qualitative interviews can also facilitate the planning of single-case evaluation studies by improving our understanding of the target problem, how to measure it, and how best to intervene. Interviews additionally help in identifying what parts of the intervention clients perceive to be most helpful, and why, and they can be used with significant others to corroborate client-reported data. Videotaping or audiotaping intervention sessions can aid in assessing intervention fidelity. Event logs completed by clients or significant others help us assess the location and timing of target problems, mediating circumstances, and extraneous events bearing on drawing causal inferences from outcome data patterns.

Many social work education programs emphasize single-subject designs in their research and practice curricula and urge students to use these designs in their eventual practice. I hope you will use these designs in your practice, but you should not set out to do so wearing rose-colored glasses. Be prepared to encounter practical obstacles to your use of these designs, obstacles such as client crises that do not allow time for developing adequate baselines, heavy caseloads that do not leave you ample time to plan or conduct this type of practice evaluation, clients who do not follow through on self-monitoring, or colleagues and supervisors who do not understand, appreciate, or support this "research stuff." You also should be prepared to encounter data patterns that are ambiguous and that therefore do not offer clear implications for practice. I say this not to discourage you from doing this sort of practice evaluation, but to help prepare you for the difficulties and frustrations it will entail. By expecting these problems, perhaps you will be less disappointed and more persistent when you experience them.

REVIEW QUESTIONS

1. The main feature of single-subject designs that can help practitioners infer whether their intervention appears to be the real cause of improvement in the target problem is:
   a. Having an A phase and a B phase
   b. Having many multiple measurement points before and after intervention begins

c. The opportunity to see if improvement occurs at any point
d. The feasibility of these designs

2. Which of the following is *not* an appropriate aim of a practitioner using a single-subject design with one particular case?
   a. To identify during assessment precipitating conditions influencing the target problem
   b. To know when a lack of progress may call for changing the intervention
   c. To generalize about the practitioner's or the intervention's effectiveness with other cases
   d. None of the above; they are all appropriate aims

3. To evaluate the effects of an environmental change, the client self-monitors his negative thoughts that have tended to lead to angry outbursts. Which of the following should be considered by the practitioner doing a single-subject evaluation with this client?
   a. Research reactivity
   b. Social desirability bias
   c. The obtrusiveness of the observation
   d. The possible use of self-monitoring at some point as a clinical tool
   e. All of the above

4. To increase the likelihood that your results are truly reflective of the target problem, and are not being influenced by measurement procedures, you should:
   a. Measure unobtrusively
   b. Use direct observation
   c. Use self-report scales
   d. Use interviews

5. If you are using a single-subject design to evaluate an intervention with an abusive parent, which of the following indicators of effectiveness would be the *least* appropriate, given the number of data points needed?
   a. Number of positive parenting behaviors
   b. Number of incidents of severe physical abuse
   c. Number of negative comments to the child
   d. Amount of time spent playing with the child

6. Which of the following statements is true about baselines in single-subject designs?

a. They should be no longer than a few measurement points.
b. They should be stable.
c. They should show that the target problem is clearly improving.
d. All of the above.

7. A practitioner obtains the following data in a single-subject evaluation of her effectiveness in using play therapy to reduce a child's nightmares.

Number of nightmares:

A phase: 3 3 2 2 1 1 0 0 0 B phase: 0 0 0 0 0 0 0 0 0

What should the practitioner conclude from these data?

a. The intervention is effective with this client.
b. The intervention is ineffective with this client.
c. Maturation or the passage of time appears to be a plausible explanation.
d. None of the above.
e. Only a and c.
f. Only b and c.

8. Suppose that in the above evaluation the practitioner obtained the following results:

Number of nightmares:

A phase: 2 2 2 2 2 0 0 0 B phase: 0 0 0 0 0 0 0 0 0

What should the practitioner conclude from these data?

a. The intervention is effective with this client.
b. The intervention is ineffective with this client.
c. History appears to be a plausible explanation.
d. None of the above.
e. Only a and c.
f. Only b and c.

9. Suppose that in the above evaluation the practitioner obtained the following results:

Number of nightmares:

A phase: 2 2 3 2 2 3 2 2 B phase: 1 0 1 0 0 0 0 0 0

What should the practitioner conclude from these data?

a. It is plausible that the intervention is effective with this client.

b. The intervention is not effective with this client.

c. History cannot be entirely ruled out.

d. None of the above.

e. Only a and c.

f. Only b and c.

10. Suppose you use an ABAB design to evaluate the effectiveness of a group intervention aimed at helping a particular child improve her social skills. Your outcome indicator is the number of friends she plays with after school each day, and you obtain the following results:

    A_1: 0 0 0 0 0 B_1: 1 1 2 2 2 A_2: 2 2 2 2 2 B_2: 2 2 2 2 2

    What should you conclude from these data?

    a. It is plausible that the intervention is effective with this client.

    b. The intervention is not effective with this client.

    c. History cannot be entirely ruled out.

    d. None of the above.

    e. Only a and c.

    f. Only b and c.

11. Suppose you conducted a multiple baseline study to evaluate the intervention in question 10. In this study you introduce three girls from the same school to the group at different points, and you obtain the following results regarding the number of friends each plays with after school each day:

	Baseline	Intervention
Girl 1	0 0 0	1 1 1 2 2 2 2
Girl 2	0 0 0 1 1	1 2 2 2 2
Girl 3	0 0 0 1 1 1 1	2 2 2

    What should you conclude from these data?

    a. It is plausible that the intervention is effective with these clients.

    b. The intervention does not appear to be effective with these clients.

    c. Generalization of effects is a plausible explanation.

    d. None of the above.

    e. Only a and c.

    f. Only b and c.

12. Suppose you used the same intervention as in questions 10 and 11, but before starting the group intervention you tried a social skills intervention with the

client in an individual context. Suppose your ABC design yielded the following results regarding number of friends she plays with after school each day:

A: 0 0 0 0 0 0   B: 0 0 0 0 0 0   C: 1 1 1 2 2 2

What should you conclude from these data?

a. It is plausible that the group intervention is effective with this client.
b. The group intervention does not appear to be effective with this client.
c. The individual intervention may be a necessary precursor to the group intervention.
d. None of the above.
e. Only a and c.
f. Only b and c.

13. In single-subject practice evaluation, replication can:
    a. Reduce ambiguity in the meaning of specific outcomes
    b. Enhance external validity
    c. Help in sorting out different alternative plausible explanations for particular data patterns
    d. All of the above

Exercises 10.1 to 10.8

Below are eight hypothetical data patterns for AB design findings in eight unrelated hypothetical practice evaluations of an intervention attempting to reduce an undesirable behavior. Develop an AB design graph for each pattern, interpret the findings, and discuss alternative explanations and whether and why the findings are ambiguous or clearcut.

EXERCISE 10.1: A: 3 2 2 3 2 2 3 3 0 0   B: 0 0 0 0 0 0 0 0 0 0

EXERCISE 10.2: A: 1 1 1 1 1 1 3 4 4 4 B: 4 3 1 1 1 1 1 1 1 1

EXERCISE 10.3: A: 4 4 4 4 4 4 3 4 5 4 B: 4 5 4 4 3 4 4 1 0 0

EXERCISE 10.4: A: 7 4 6 3 5 3 5 2 4 1 B: 4 1 4 0 3 1 3 0 2 0

EXERCISE 10.5: A: 2 1 2 1 2 2 7 8 7 8 B: 2 1 2 0 1 2 8 2 1 1

EXERCISE 10.6: A: 3 4 3 4 3 4 3 4 3 3 B: 6 8 5 1 0 0 1 0 0 0

EXERCISE 10.7: A: 7 7 7 6 6 6 5 5 4 4 B: 3 3 3 2 2 2 1 1 0 0

EXERCISE 10.8: A: 5 5 4 4 6 5 4 5 6 5 B: 2 1 2 1 0 1 1 0 1 0

EXERCISE 10.9

On a separate page prepare an event log to be completed by clients and/or significant others for a hypothetical single-case evaluation study you make up, based, if possible, on a real case you have worked with in your field practicum or elsewhere.

DISCUSSION QUESTIONS

1. Suppose the data in Exercises 10.1 to 10.8, above, represented eight separate studies on the same intervention with the same target problem. Discuss how you would aggregate the findings of the eight studies, and interpret the aggregate findings in terms of their implications for the effectiveness of the intervention.

2. Do you think that you are likely to conduct single-subject evaluations as part of your professional social work practice? Why or why not?

3. Do you think single-subject designs are applicable primarily to practitioners using behavioral interventions and not very useful for practitioners using nonbehavioral interventions? Why or why not?

4. Explain the core logic of single-subject designs, and discuss with respect to that logic the relative degree of internal validity of AB designs with very few data points, AB designs with many data points, ABAB designs, and multiple-baseline designs.

5. Discuss the advantages of incorporating qualitative methods—such as interviews, videotaping or audiotaping, and event logs—as part of single-case evaluation studies.

CHAPTER

Survey Research

OBJECTIVES

1. Identify two advantages and two disadvantages of using surveys as a mode of observation.
2. Identify two types of surveys commonly conducted in social work agencies.
3. Identify two advantages of using self-administered questionnaires in surveys.
4. Describe three methods for promoting higher response rates in mailed surveys.
5. Describe the function and process of monitoring mailed questionnaires.
6. Prepare an effective cover letter for a mailed survey.
7. Discuss the importance of nonresponse in mailed surveys and identify response rates that are generally considered adequate, good, and very good.
8. Identify four advantages of interviews over questionnaires.
9. Describe five general rules for survey interviewing.
10. Identify three advantages and two disadvantages of telephone surveys, as compared to face-to-face surveys.
11. Describe the functions and risks associated with secondary analysis.

PRACTICE-RELEVANT SUMMARY

Surveys are a data collection method in which a sample of respondents is interviewed or administered questionnaires. Surveys have been conducted since ancient times and are one of the most frequently used modes of observation in social work and the social sciences. Surveys offer an expedient way to collect data describing populations. Surveys can be used for exploratory and explanatory as well as descriptive purposes. They can be cross-sectional or longitudinal. Individuals are the most common units of analysis, but not the only ones.

Due largely to the feasibility of surveys, and their relevance to some important concerns of social work agencies, social work practitioners—particularly those in administrative or planning positions—often find themselves involved in conducting surveys. Common foci of agency surveys are the satisfaction of their clients with the services they have received and the needs of current and prospective clients for new services being planned.

The use of self-administered questionnaires is one of the most expedient ways to conduct a survey. Self-administered questionnaires are relatively inexpensive and take relatively little time to administer. Another advantage is that they give respondents complete anonymity, which might be important when sensitive topics are covered. The mailed survey method is the one most commonly used with self-administered questionnaires.

A key factor influencing the representativeness—and hence the value—of mailed surveys is the response rate. Several methods can be used to encourage higher response rates. One is the use of a self-mailing questionnaire requiring no return envelope. If that is not feasible, you can use stamped, self-addressed return envelopes. A cover letter should explain the importance of the survey, express the endorsement of esteemed sponsors, guarantee anonymity to respondents and explain how they were selected, and indicate how long the questionnaire takes to complete. Shorter questionnaires are more likely to be returned than longer ones.

It is important to monitor the returns of questionnaires. As the rate of return starts dropping off, a follow-up mailing should occur. It is a good idea to plan on two follow-up mailings, two or three weeks apart. It is best to send a new copy of the questionnaire with each follow-up letter of encouragement.

The higher the response rate, the greater the likelihood that the sample is representative of the population. No strict, precise standards exist to help you determine whether your response rate is acceptable. Rules of thumb, however, are commonly used, which depict 50% as an adequate response rate, 60% as a good response rate, and 70% as a very good response rate.

Interviews offer some advantages over self-administered questionnaires. One is that they decrease the likelihood of obtaining incomplete questionnaires or of respondents tossing questionnaires into the wastebasket. Another is the opportunity they provide for explaining words that respondents do not understand. This decreases the number of "don't know" and "no answer" responses. Interviews also make observing social situations and probing into unexpected responses possible.

Interviewers should dress in a fashion similar to that of the people being interviewed. They should be neat and clean. They should have a pleasant demeanor. They should be familiar with the questionnaire, be able to read items naturally and smoothly, follow the question wording exactly, and record responses exactly. They should know how to probe, in a neutral fashion, when asking open-ended questions or when inappropriate replies are given to close-ended questions. Interviewers should be trained thoroughly and supervised, and they should be given specifications to help explain and clarify difficulties that may arise with specific items.

Interview surveys can be conducted face to face or by telephone. During the Depression era telephone interviews were found to be dubious because there were many more poor people without telephones. This produced biased samples—most notoriously in 1936, when a telephone survey predicted that Alf Landon would win a landslide victory over Franklin Roosevelt in the presidential election. Today, however, only about 3% of all households are without telephones. Class-related biases connected to unlisted numbers can be avoided by using random-digit dialing. Hence there is much less class bias in telephone surveys nowadays. Telephone interviews are more acceptable today and offer some important advantages over face-to-face interviews.

They are cheaper and quicker, since no travel is involved. They avoid the problem of how to dress and may be safer for interviewers. Not having to face the interviewer in person may facilitate more honesty in giving socially disapproved answers. On the other hand, telephone interviews also have some disadvantages. They may increase suspicion among some respondents, especially those who have become alienated by the proliferation of manipulative telephone sales solicitations. Reluctant respondents may find it easier to stop the interview by hanging up.

Surveys have some disadvantages as compared to alternative modes of observation. Their need for standardization can result in inflexibility, which can limit the opportunity to assess deeper meanings and unique social situations. Survey data, therefore, can appear superficial and artificial. Moreover, surveys only assess what people say, which may not match what they do. These disadvantages can be offset by combining a qualitative inquiry with a survey.

Surveys have some special strengths that other modes of observation may lack. They make it feasible to gather data from a large sample and generalize to a large population (assuming proper sampling and survey procedures are used). A weakness of surveys can also be a strength. Their standardization and inflexibility can make surveys less vulnerable to biases in observation and data collection than some other modes of observation. This is accomplished by requiring that questions be asked the same way with all respondents and that inappropriate meanings not be imputed to responses.

Despite the relative expediency of most surveys, not every social worker in need of survey data will have the means to conduct a survey. This is particularly true regarding large-scale surveys. One alternative is to conduct a secondary analysis of survey data previously conducted by others. This has become easier with the growth of computerized databases offered by various state and national agencies and accessible on the Internet. Secondary analyses of these databases can be done rapidly and inexpensively. However, secondary analysis can also involve a risk regarding validity. The way questions were asked in generating the original database may not be a valid measure of what you have in mind.

REVIEW QUESTIONS

1. Which of the following is a disadvantage of survey research in data collection?
   a. Increased flexibility
   b. Greater vulnerability to bias
   c. Reduced feasibility to obtain large samples
   d. All of the above
   e. None of the above

2. Social work agencies commonly conduct surveys to:
   a. Assess client satisfaction with or needs for services
   b. Determine whether services are causing desired outcomes

c. Assess the deeper meanings of client problems or needs

d. All of the above

3. Which of the following is *not* an advantage of using self-administered questionnaires in surveys?

   a. Lowered costs

   b. Less reluctance by respondents to answer questions about sensitive issues

   c. Less nonresponse bias

   d. Less time required to collect data

4. Higher response rates in mailed surveys can be promoted by:

   a. Using self-mailing questionnaires requiring no return envelopes

   b. Enclosing cover letters explaining the importance and sponsorship of the survey

   c. Using shorter questionnaires

   d. Having follow-up mailings

   e. All of the above

5. A 50% response rate to a mailed survey is generally considered:

   a. Too small

   b. Adequate

   c. Good

   d. Very good

6. Which of the following is *not* an advantage of interviews over questionnaires?

   a. Higher response rates

   b. Fewer items unanswered

   c. More opportunity to probe into unexpected responses

   d. Less reluctance by respondents to answer questions about sensitive issues

7. Which of the following is *not* a good rule for survey interviewing?

   a. Dress as you usually dress; don't try to dress like your respondents.

   b. Don't read questionnaire items verbatim; rephrase questions in your own words.

   c. Summarize or paraphrase respondent answers that could be worded more clearly or with better grammar.

   d. When probing into unclear responses, ask if the respondent meant what you think they meant.

   e. All of the above (they are all things *not* to do).

   f. None of the above (they are all good rules).

8. Which of the following is *not* an advantage of telephone surveys over face-to-face surveys?
   a. They are cheaper and quicker.
   b. They avoid the problem of how to dress.
   c. They may facilitate more honesty in giving socially disapproved answers.
   d. They make it harder for respondents to prematurely terminate the interview.
   e. None of the above; all are advantages.

9. Which of the following is *not* true about secondary analysis?
   a. Because the data were already gathered, you don't have to worry about measurement problems like validity.
   b. It can be done more rapidly and inexpensively than surveys.
   c. The number of databases available for secondary analysis is growing.
   d. None of the above; all are advantages.

10. Which of the following statements is true about survey response rates?
    a. A demonstrated lack of response bias is more important than a high response rate.
    b. Anything less than 80% is not considered a good response rate.
    c. If people don't respond to your first mailing, they probably will not respond to follow-up mailings.
    d. All of the above.
    e. None of the above.

EXERCISE 11.1

Prepare a cover letter for a hypothetical survey on consumer satisfaction in your agency.

EXERCISE 11.2

Prepare several open-ended questions about student satisfaction with their social work courses. Form a group of three students and take turns interviewing each other with the questions you've prepared. Have a third person observe and critique each interview, then engage in a three-way discussion of each interview. Focus on how well you utilize neutral probes in this exercise.

EXERCISE 11.3

Repeat Exercise 11.2, this time focusing on how well you record responses. Both the interviewer and the observer should record responses. Compare each pair of recordings, and discuss how to improve each of the recordings from the standpoint of the principles discussed in Chapter 11.

EXERCISE 11.4

Suppose you are interested in estimating the number of women in your city who need services for battered women but who are reluctant to use those services. You do not have the resources to conduct a survey, but you can conduct a secondary analysis of data collected by a local planning agency in a survey involving face-to-face interviews of a large sample of women randomly selected from a list of residential addresses in your city. The interviews covered a wide range of women's issues, including questions about whether they were involved in an abusive relationship. Discuss the advantages and disadvantages of basing your estimate on a secondary analysis of this source of data.

DISCUSSION QUESTIONS

1. How do you react when you receive telephone calls asking you to respond to a telephone survey? Under what conditions do you choose to respond or not respond? What have interviewers said or done that influenced you to respond, not respond, or perhaps abort the interview?

2. Suppose you conducted a mailed survey on a sensitive topic and, despite implementing all the recommended efforts to maximize response rates, were only able to obtain a 25% response rate. How would you characterize the value of your data, and what issues would you consider in forming your judgment? What additional steps could you take to assess the value of your data?

3. Make a list of at least four research questions that might be of great interest to social workers in a particular agency. Include at least one question that would best fit each of the following survey modalities: a mailed survey, a face-to-face interview survey, and a telephone survey. Also include at least one question that would best be addressed by a modality other than a survey. Discuss why each question best fits the particular modality you've identified for it.

CHAPTER

Qualitative Research Methods

OBJECTIVES

1. Describe the use of grounded theory and give an example of how it could be used to study a social work research problem.
2. Describe the use of ethnography and give an example of how it could be used to study a social work research problem.
3. Discuss how the use of grounded theory, ethnography, and phenomenology can overlap.
4. Contrast and identify the advantages and disadvantages of observing as a complete participant, as a participant-as-observer, and as a complete observer.
5. Describe the dilemma involved in attempting to balance the competing aims of maintaining objectivity and adopting an alien point of view in qualitative research.
6. Identify the steps involved in preparing to undertake direct observation in the field.
7. Discuss how the aims of sampling in field research differ from the aims of sampling in quantitative research, and describe the purpose and illustrate the use of snowball sampling, deviant case sampling, intensity sampling, critical incidents sampling, maximum variation sampling, homogeneous sampling, and theoretical sampling.
8. Discuss the ways qualitative interviewing differs from survey interviewing, and identify the differences between the following three forms of qualitative interviewing: informal conversational interviews, interview guides, and standardized open-ended interviews.
9. Identify the tools and strategies field researchers employ to manage the challenging process of recording observations and maximizing the quality of the recorded notes.
10. Describe the following techniques field researchers have developed for processing qualitative data: rewriting your notes, creating files, and using computers.
11. Describe the guidelines for looking for similarities and dissimilarities and for detecting patterns in the analysis of qualitative data.
12. Identify and define seven logical errors commonly made in qualitative data analysis.
13. Describe the case study method and illustrate how it may be applied to a social work research topic.

14. Discuss the key strengths and weaknesses of field research, particularly as they pertain to depth of understanding, subjectivity, generalizability, and research ethics.

PRACTICE-RELEVANT SUMMARY

As this *Study Guide* is being written, politicians across the United States appear to be moving toward enacting legislation that will include features like limiting to two years the welfare eligibility of mothers and children receiving Aid to Families with Dependent Children (AFDC) and refusing payments for children born after the mother is already on welfare. Social workers whose practice involves policy analysis and advocacy are terribly concerned about the impact this impending legislation will have on mothers and children whose AFDC benefits will be terminated. What will the mothers resort to in order to survive (assuming that a shortage of jobs that they qualify for and a shortage of affordable child care will make it hard for them to become legitimate wage earners)? What impact will this have on their ability to mother their children? What impact will the deterioration in mothering and the loss of subsistence resources have on the children? Will they become homeless? Will they be starving and freezing on the streets? Will they and their mothers increasingly resort to crime? What impact will all this have on the type of adults they become, assuming they live that long?

It is perhaps impossible to anticipate all, or even most, of the important ways the impending legislation can change the lives of AFDC recipients. What research methods can social workers use to study this phenomenon and inform the public about the impact of the legislation? Experiments will be difficult, since we don't control the independent variable, which is the variation in welfare policy. Surveys are possible, but is it reasonable to expect an acceptable level of participation in a survey? More important, perhaps, can we foresee the future ways this legislation is likely to impact the lives of welfare recipients well enough to know all the questions we should ask and how we should ask them? Neither experimental nor survey data, moreover, are apt to tug at the heartstrings of an electorate that somehow has come to believe that AFDC is a central cause of many social ills and budget deficits. Another kind of data is needed to do that, data that help the reader walk in the shoes of good people who are suffering. At times like these, therefore, it is easier to see the relevance to social work practitioners of learning about qualitative research methods, since qualitative research methods help us study new phenomena that we cannot adequately anticipate, and empathize with the lives of people through observations that cannot, and perhaps should not, be reduced to numbers.

Essentially all of qualitative inquiry is based on the *grounded theory* method. This approach is an inductive process of seeking patterns in one set of observations and then engaging in a constant comparison process of seeking different types of cases and observations and constantly modifying working hypotheses until a point is reached when new types of cases and observations no longer alter the findings.

Qualitative research is often called *naturalistic research,* to convey the emphasis of observing everyday life as it unfolds in its natural environment. It is also often called *ethnography* or *ethnographic research,* since it often involves studying a culture from the point of view of the inhabitants of that culture. Key elements in an ethnographic research strategy include establishing generic propositions, being open to inquiring about anything, trying to see the world through the eyes of the people you seek to understand and gain deep familiarity with them, using the grounded theory approach, assuming that there is a true reality, constantly aiming for new observations and new analyses, and balancing the use of observations and theoretical elaboration in presenting data.

Phenomenology is a term used to convey the qualitative researcher's focus on people's subjective experiences and interpretations. Phenomenology can involve heuristic inquiry, in which researchers shed efforts to be detached observers and instead experience a phenomenon firsthand. The process of attempting to detect patterns from voluminous details is called *hermeneutics*. *Verstehen* is a German term for attempting to understand those we observe from their own perspective.

Qualitative research is often called *field research*. Field research typically involves participant observation, which can be conducted on a continuum from complete participant to complete observer, with less extreme options of participant-as-observer and observer-as-participant in between. At one extreme, the complete participant may be best able to fully grasp what it's like to be the people under study but may also be most vulnerable to affecting what is being studied and to lose one's own sense of identity and analytic stance. At the other extreme, complete observers preserve their sense of identity and analytic stance and are less likely to affect what is being studied but are also less likely to develop a full appreciation of what is being studied. When operating toward the complete-participant end of the continuum, researchers should try to achieve a difficult balance between adopting the points of view of the people they are studying and being able to step outside those viewpoints and analyzing them from the standpoint of an objective social scientist.

The field researcher prepares for the field by reviewing literature on the group to be studied, discussing the group with informant members of the group, and developing rapport with group members. Then sampling decisions must be made, typically involving nonprobability sampling techniques that incorporate aspects of *quota sampling* and *purposive sampling*. *Snowball sampling* is also commonly used; this approach begins by identifying a few relevant subjects and expands the sample through referrals from those subjects. *Deviant case sampling* is useful, too, since important insights can be gained from studying people who do not fit the usual pattern. *Intensity sampling* helps prevent a distorted portrayal of the phenomenon by selecting cases that are more or less intense than usual but not so unusual that they would be called deviant. Another useful strategy is *critical incidents sampling*, studying events in which something of special importance seemed to happen. *Maximum variation sampling* calls for studying a phenomenon under heterogeneous conditions to capture its diversity. *Homogeneous sampling*, on the other hand, is a strategy for studying those subjects or events thought most likely to evince a particular construct of interest. When using grounded theory, *theoretical sampling* comes into play, as described above with regard to the constant comparison method of grounded theory.

In addition to direct observation, qualitative research relies heavily on open-ended interviewing that tends to be unstructured. At one extreme are completely unstructured *informal conversational interviews* that contain no predetermined questions and in which you can use your social work listening, probing, and attending skills to subtly direct the flow of the conversation to stay on track and help you develop a richer understanding of things relevant to your research. At the other extreme are *standardized open-ended interviews,* in which open-ended questions are written out in advance precisely as they are to be asked during the interview. In between the two extremes is the *interview guide* approach, which lists the topics and issues to be covered in outline form and allows the interviewer to adapt the sequencing and wording of questions to each particular interview.

Other qualitative methods frequently mentioned in the literature that may employ observation or interviewing include *case studies, client logs,* and *life histories.*

Respondent answers to interview questions should be recorded as fully as possible. Verbatim recording is ideal, with a tape recorder when applicable. Additional penciled notes should be recorded in a notebook at the scene of action or as soon as possible afterward. Notes should include both exact descriptions of what happened and your interpretations of them. Since you will be unable to write down everything you observe, you should use your judgment to record the most important things. You should take notes in stages, beginning with sketchy notes at the scene of action and then rewriting them in more detail as soon as you are alone.

Notes should be retyped each night, with multiple copies made for cutting and pasting later. Notes should be organized into files containing a chronological record, historical and biographical files, a bibliographical file, and analytic files. Many types of analytic files can be created in a continuous, flexible process.

Computers can be used to process qualitative data, using word processing systems and numerous programs designed specifically for use in qualitative research. In analyzing qualitative data, you should look for similarities and dissimilarities across groupings of observations, patterns of interaction and events, and norms of behavior and deviation from general norms. Things to look for in attempting to discern patterns include *frequencies, magnitudes, structures, processes, causes,* and *consequences.*

You can try to avoid the danger of looking only for patterns that support your theoretical predilections by augmenting your qualitative observations with quantitative ones, seeing if colleagues independently discern the same patterns, and using introspection. Logical pitfalls to keep in mind, and to try to avoid, in drawing conclusions include *provincialism, going native, emotional reactions, hasty conclusions, questionable cause, suppressed evidence,* and *false dilemma.*

The chief strength of qualitative research is the depth of understanding that it permits. Another key advantage is its flexibility. It also can be relatively inexpensive, although this is not always the case. The chief weaknesses of qualitative research are its vulnerability to the subjectivity of the researchers and those being observed and its limited generalizability. Field research, by bringing researchers into direct and often intimate contact with their subjects, also can raise ethical concerns dramatically.

REVIEW QUESTIONS

1. Qualitative research methods are more appropriate than quantitative methods for:
   a. Studying new phenomena that we cannot anticipate
   b. Developing a deeper understanding of meanings

c. Situations that require a flexible research approach
d. All of the above
e. None of the above

2. The grounded theory method:
   a. Starts with theory, then seeks observations to confirm it
   b. Is an inductive process for letting theory emerge from observational patterns
   c. Excludes methods involving observations or interviews
   d. Is a geological social work method

3. Which of the following is a term often used to characterize qualitative research?
   a. Ethnography
   b. Phenomenology
   c. Naturalistic research
   d. All of the above
   e. None of the above

4. The complete-participant strategy of observation has the advantage of:
   a. Helping the researcher fully grasp what it's like to be the people under study
   b. Helping the research avoid affecting what is being studied
   c. Helping researchers preserve their sense of identity and analytic stance
   d. All of the above
   e. None of the above

5. Researchers using the complete-participant strategy of observation are less likely to:
   a. Develop a full appreciation of what is being studied
   b. Affect what is being studied
   c. Preserve their sense of identity and analytic stance
   d. Encounter ethical constraints

6. Complete-participant researchers should:
   a. Never step outside the viewpoints of their subjects
   b. Never adopt the viewpoints of their subjects
   c. Try to both adopt the viewpoints of their subjects and be able to step outside them
   d. Avoid the standpoint of the objective social scientist

7. The field researcher prepares for the field by:
   a. Reviewing literature on the group to be studied
   b. Discussing the group with informant members of the group

c. Developing rapport with group members
d. All of the above
e. None of the above

8. Which of the following is *not* a common sampling technique frequently employed in qualitative research?
a. Snowball sampling
b. Deviant case sampling
c. Intensity sampling
d. Critical incidents sampling
e. Stratified random sampling

9. Which of the following is *not* true about qualitative interviewing?
a. It tends to be less structured than quantitative interviewing.
b. It tends to be open-ended.
c. It may involve informal conversational interviews that contain no predetermined questions.
d. It never involves asking questions precisely as they are written out in advance.

10. When recording qualitative data, you should:
a. Record responses to interview questions verbatim
b. Describe what happens as well as your interpretations of what you observe
c. Record at the scene of action and rewrite your notes in more detail as soon as you are alone
d. All of the above
e. None of the above

11. Field notes should be organized into:
a. Historical and biographical files
b. Bibliographical files
c. Analytic files
d. All of the above

12. Which of the following is true about analyzing qualitative data?
a. Because the data are not quantitative, computer processing is unlikely to be applicable.
b. You should look for similarities and dissimilarities across groupings of observations.
c. You should look only for those patterns that fit your theoretical orientation.

d. Quantitative indicators should not be included.
e. All of the above.

13. When analyzing qualitative data, you should try to:
    a. Interpret the data in terms of your own point of view
    b. Identify exclusively with the point of view of the people you've studied
    c. Allow your emotional reactions to the data to influence your data analysis
    d. Select only one interpretation; do not recognize the plausibility of multiple interpretations
    e. All of the above
    f. None of the above

14. Which of the following is a chief strength of qualitative research?
    a. Depth of understanding
    b. Tightly structured methods
    c. Measurement objectivity
    d. Generalizability

EXERCISE 12.1

In the social work courses you are taking this semester, observe and take field notes on the social interactions among social work students and their instructors ten minutes before and ten minutes after your next class session in each course. The focus of your inquiry should be on the nature of verbal and nonverbal communication among students and between students and instructors and on how the communication varies depending on such factors as the instructor's presence or absence, who is communicating with whom, and the instructor's subject area (that is, research, policy, practice, and so on).

Follow the guidelines in Chapter 12 in the section on "Recording Observations," including separate notes on empirical observations and on interpretations of them. Then develop your research conclusions and write them below. Have your classmates share their conclusions with each other after they all finish the exercise. Do their conclusions agree? Disagree? To what do you attribute any disagreements? (Enter your conclusions about disagreements below as well.)

EXERCISE 12.2

Prepare a set of about ten open-ended questions about student satisfaction with your social work education program. Conduct a structured interview with one or more other social work students, asking the questions exactly as you have written them out. Have another student in your class independently conduct informal conversational interviews with the same students. Both you and the other interviewer should independently record and analyze your interview data as recommended in Chapter 12. After each of you has completed your data analysis and written your conclusions, compare the similarities and differences in your conclusions and brainstorm with each other as to explanations for why the two different interview methods yielded similar or different conclusions. In your discussion, be sure to consider potential limitations and logical pitfalls that might account for some of your conclusions or some of the differences between the two sets of conclusions.

EXERCISE 12.3

Write down the logical pitfall for each of the following hypothetical situations. Compare your answers with those of your classmates and discuss any differences you encounter.

a. A 22-year-old social worker who continues to grapple with issues connected to her perception that her parents were overprotective of her tends to interpret the behavior of the troubled adolescents she observes in terms of their reactions to parental overprotection.

b. A social worker seeking to understand the culture of residents in a juvenile correctional facility begins to see the world through the eyes of the residents, which includes disregarding the viewpoints of the security staff and other authority figures, based exclusively on the horror stories he hears about them from the residents.

c. A social worker who recently had to place her elderly parent in a nursing home becomes angry when conducting observations of staff-resident interactions in a study of nursing home care. She begins to focus exclusively, and in a moralistic manner, on staff inadequacies.

d. A social worker observing social behavior in a prison cafeteria observes that all the white prisoners eat on one side of the room and all the African American prisoners eat on the other side. He therefore concludes that the prison staff practice racist segregation.

e. Another social worker interviewing the prisoners in situation d, above, learns that each group prefers to eat on its own side of the room. Based on this, she concludes that racism is not a problem among the prison staff.

EXERCISE 12.4

Practice the preparation of a client log by preparing one for yourself. Use it to monitor the occurrence of a behavior you would like to change (for example, smoking, overeating, and so forth). Record critical incidents and related information as described in the "Client Logs" section of Chapter 12. Compare your log with the logs of your classmates.

DISCUSSION QUESTIONS

1. Do you think you would have a preference regarding doing qualitative versus quantitative research? If so, which approach would you prefer and why? Be sure to consider methodological issues as well as your own style in formulating your answer.

2. Discuss the benefits of gathering quantitative data to augment your qualitative data.

3. Discuss how ethnographic researchers can attempt to adopt the points of view of the people they are studying, while at the same time preserving their scientific objectivity and analytic stance.

4. In light of the superior generalizability of findings based on probability sampling techniques, discuss the reasons nonprobability sampling techniques are usually preferrable when conducting qualitative research.

CHAPTER

Unobtrusive Research: Quantitative and Qualitative Methods

OBJECTIVES

1. Define unobtrusive observation and distinguish it from obtrusive observation.
2. Identify the advantages of unobtrusive observation and illustrate its application to a social work research question.
3. Describe content analysis and illustrate its use in investigating research questions about social work practice.
4. Provide an example of content analysis in social work in which the unit of analysis differs from the unit of observation.
5. Illustrate how sampling techniques are applied in content analysis.
6. Distinguish manifest and latent content coding and provide examples of each.
7. Provide an example in which a quantitative count of manifest content categories would not translate into a precise depiction of the degree to which a particular concept characterizes content.
8. Identify three guidelines for counting and recordkeeping in content analysis.
9. Distinguish qualitative and quantitative approaches to content analysis and provide an example of each in social work.
10. Identify the strengths and weaknesses of content analysis.
11. Explain why social workers seeking to analyze existing statistics should be concerned with, and should inquire as to, their reliability and validity.
12. Provide an example of analyzing existing statistics to research social welfare policy, and identify three sources of existing statistics for policy research.
13. Distinguish qualitative historical/comparative methods, such as *verstehen* and hermeneutics, from quantitatively oriented longitudinal methods.
14. Identify three sources of historical/comparative data.
15. Distinguish primary and secondary sources of historical/comparative data, and discuss the cautions that are advisable in working with each type of source.
16. Discuss the importance of corroboration in historical research.

PRACTICE-RELEVANT SUMMARY

Observation in social work practice and research tends to be obtrusive—that is, it tends to be conducted with the awareness of the people being assessed that they are being observed. Obtrusive observation can yield misleading information, because it may influence what people say or do. Obtrusive observation also involves collecting data in the present and can be relatively time consuming. To avoid some of these problems, you might wish to conduct unobtrusive analyses of available records, such as agency documents, case records, media reports, professional literature, and so on. This will enable you to study phenomena that have already occurred, which may save you time and will not involve the people being assessed in the measurement process.

One prime unobtrusive method is *content analysis,* which can be applied to available records or virtually any other form of human communication. It consists primarily of coding and tabulating the occurrences of certain forms of content that are being communicated. Content analysis has been an important source of social work practice knowledge, such as when a content analysis of excerpts from practitioner-client sessions identified the core conditions of a helping relationship (that is, empathy, warmth, genuineness, and so on).

Sampling is an important feature of content analysis: virtually any conventional sampling technique can be employed. One reason for the importance of sampling in content analysis is the complexity involved, since the unit of analysis often differs from the unit of observation.

Content analysis is essentially a coding operation and involves logical issues in conceptualization and operationalization as were discussed in Chapter 5. An important distinction in this connection is between manifest and latent coding. *Manifest coding* is a strictly quantitative method for counting the number of times certain words are used. *Latent coding* is more qualitative; it assesses the overall meaning of a passage or document. Quantitative counts of manifest content categories do not translate into precise depictions of the degree to which a particular concept characterizes a document's content. For example, if one agency's board meeting minutes mention cultural diversity twice as often as a second agency's, that doesn't necessarily mean that the first agency's committment to cultural diversity is double the second agency's commitment.

When conducting a quantitative content analysis, it is important to use numerical codes that clearly distinguish between your units of analysis and your units of observation. Usually it is important to record the base from which the counting is done. Thus, rather than just say that *cultural diversity* was mentioned 20 times in one document and 10 times in another, you should also indicate the word length of each document. Issues of *validity* and *reliability* are noteworthy in content analysis. In quantitative content analysis, the number of times a word or phrase appears may not be a valid indicator of the degree to which a document has a particular attribute. Qualitative content analysis may be better at tapping underlying meanings, but different coders might have different judgments about the latent meaning of content.

Existing statistics provide another source for unobtrusive research. There are many sources for existing statistics in social work research, such as those issued annually by government and private agencies dealing with social problems. A challenge is to find existing data that cover what you are interested in. Often the data may pertain in some way to your interest but might not be an exact, valid representation of the variables you want to draw conclusions about. You should also look into potential biases or carelessness in the way the statistics were originally gathered and reported. Don't assume that because they are official documents, they are necessarily reliable or valid.

Historical/comparative analysis, which is usually done qualitatively, is a method for tracing developments over time and comparing developmental processes across cultures. A main focus is on seeking to discover common patterns that recur in different times and places. In social work research, for example, one can see recurring patterns over time in welfare policy reform efforts and mental health policy reform efforts. Noble reforms proposed in ways that would cost taxpayers more money fail again and again because they get adopted and implemented with insufficient public funding to implement critical features of the proposed reforms.

Endless sources are possible for historical/comparative analysis, such as letters, diaries, lectures, newspapers, magazines, agency documents and annual reports, and so on. *Primary sources* provide firsthand accounts by someone present at an event. *Secondary sources* describe past phenomena based on primary sources. People who author primary sources may depict events in a biased manner, due to their vested interests, and historical/comparative researchers should vigilantly consider and look into this possibility. A prime way to handle this problem is by looking for corroboration across multiple sources.

Historical/comparative research involves primarily fluid, qualitative interpretive methods, such as *verstehen* and hermeneutics, which do not contain easily listed steps to follow. The historical/comparative researcher seeks to detect patterns in voluminous details and to take on, mentally, the circumstances, views, and feelings of those being studied and to interpret their actions appropriately.

REVIEW QUESTIONS

1. When we conduct unobtrusive observation:
   a. People are aware that they are being observed.
   b. We can influence what our subjects say or do.
   c. We collect data only in the present time.
   d. All of the above.
   e. None of the above.

2. Which of the following is an example of unobtrusive observation of cultural diversity in an agency?
   a. Count the proportion of staff, board members, and clients of each background as depicted in agency documents and client records.
   b. Interview staff about their views regarding cultural diversity.

c. Obtain the consent of administrators and practitioners to attend agency meetings to observe how often cultural diversity is discussed.

d. All of the above.

3. A content analysis is conducted of individual client case records to see if agencies that have provided more in-service training on cultural diversity appear to provide services that are more ethnically sensitive than agencies offering less in-service training on cultural diversity. Which of the following statements is true about this content analysis?

   a. Individual case records are the units of observation.

   b. Individual agencies are the units of analysis.

   c. Individual case records are the units of analysis.

   d. Individual agencies are the units of observation.

   e. None of the above.

   f. Both a and b, only, are true.

   g. Both c and d, only, are true.

4. In the content analysis in question 3 above, the researcher read each session's progress notes and made an overall assessment of whether it reflected ethnic sensitivity. The researcher was doing:

   a. Latent content coding

   b. Manifest content coding

   c. Quantitative coding

   d. Reliability coding

5. An agency administrator, concerned about the extent to which her staff are taking their clients' ethnicity into account when providing services, conducts a content analysis of staff progress notes and finds that staff with social work degrees mentioned the client's ethnicity 100 times, whereas staff with other degrees mentioned it 50 times. The administrator was correct in concluding:

   a. Social workers are twice as likely as other staff to take ethnicity into account.

   b. Other staff are half as likely as social workers to take ethnicity into account.

   c. Ethnicity was mentioned more times in social workers' progress notes than in the progress notes of other staff.

   d. All of the above.

6. If textbook A on social work practice mentions client ethnicity 100 times and textbook B mentions it 90 times, then:

   a. Textbook A emphasizes ethnicity more than textbook B.

   b. Textbook A devotes a greater proportion of content to ethnicity.

   c. Both a and b are true.

   d. Neither a nor b is necessarily true.

7. As compared to latent coding, manifest coding in content analysis:
   a. Has an advantage in terms of validity
   b. Is less suitable for tapping underlying meanings
   c. Has a disadvantage in terms of reliability
   d. Has less specificity
   e. None of the above

8. Which of the following is/are true about using existing statistics issued in official agency statistical reports?
   a. We can be reasonably certain that their reliability and validity are high.
   b. The data may have been collected in a careless fashion.
   c. Biases may have influenced the way data were collected and reported.
   d. We can be reasonably certain that the data are almost never grossly inaccurate.
   e. Both a and d, only, are true.
   f. Both b and c, only, are true.

9. In conducting a historical/comparative analysis of an agency's commitment to cultural diversity, a social worker finds that the agency's administrative minutes and letters written by the agency's executive director during the last decade express much more commitment to increasing cultural diversity in the agency than do letters and minutes from the past. Which of the following statements is/are true about this example?
   a. The minutes and letters are secondary sources.
   b. It is safe to conclude that the agency has increased its cultural diversity during the last decade.
   c. Other types of sources of data reflecting the agency's commitment to cultural diversity should be compared to the above sources to check for inaccuracies due to biases.
   d. All of the above.

10. Which of the following statements is *not* true about historical/comparative research, such as *verstehen* and hermeneutics?
   a. It involves a series of specific procedures that should be followed precisely.
   b. It involves primarily fluid, qualitative interpretive methods.
   c. It involves the detection of patterns in voluminous details.

d. It involves seeking to mentally take on the views and feelings of those being studied.

e. None of the above; they are all true.

EXERCISE 13.1

Conduct a content analysis of the chapters you have read so far in the Rubin and Babbie textbook, based on the book's latent content, to determine the extent to which the book values qualitative methods and quantitative methods equally or the extent to which it values one more than the other. I suggest you begin by skimming each chapter quickly to jog your memory, jotting brief notes as to what you would conclude about the research question in light of what you recall was said about the relative importance of qualitative or quantitative methods in each chapter. Then consider your notes qualitatively in terms of what you think the book's overall, underlying message is about the relative importance of the two sets of methods. Enter your notes and conclusions below.

EXERCISE 13.2

Once you have completed the above qualitative analysis of latent content, conduct a quantitative analysis of the same chapters with regard to their manifest content concerning the same research question. Begin by formulating a sampling plan, such as rereading every 10th or 20th page of the chapters you have already completed. Alternatively, you may want to just reread the "Main Points" listed at the end of each chapter. You will also need to conceptualize the words or phrases you will look for and count to indicate how much content on qualitative methods is in the book versus how much content on quantitative methods there is. Then proceed with your counting, recording your findings and conclusions below. Also identify below your sampling procedure and the words or phrases you looked for. (Writing this down now will be useful when you compare your findings with those of your classmates in Exercise 13.4.)

EXERCISE 13.3

Compare your conclusions in the above two exercises. Were they the same? Discuss why you think they were or were not the same. Which of the two content analyses do you think is the more valid for this particular book and *Study Guide*? Why?

EXERCISE 13.4

Compare your results and conclusions for the above two content analyses with those of your classmates. Was there more agreement among you with one approach (manifest versus latent) than the other? What do you think explains the consistency or inconsistency of results and conclusions across the students performing this exercise? What does this suggest regarding the reliability and validity of the two approaches?

DISCUSSION QUESTIONS

1. Explain why content analyses that examine both manifest and latent content may reach more valuable conclusions than content analyses restricted to only one of the two types of content.

2. Suppose you studied trends in the frequency of reported spouse abuse and reported service utilization connected to spouse abuse by analyzing two sets of existing statistics: one issued annually by a government agency and one issued annually by the National Organization for Women (NOW). In what ways, if any, do you think the government agency statistics might differ from the NOW statistics, and why? What does this imply about issues regarding the reliability and validity of existing statistics?

3. Suppose your colleague conducted the study in question 2 above and found a huge increase in the frequency of reported spouse abuse and reported service utilization connected to spouse abuse beginning in 1995 (coinciding with the start of the infamous O. J. Simpson trial). Suppose your colleague concluded that spouse abuse is on the rise, as is seeking services connected to it. After reading a rough draft of her preliminary report, which she gave you in the hope of getting your feedback, what would you say to your colleague regarding whether her conclusions about the increase are warranted in light of the validity of the statistics she used as a measure of the rate of actual spouse abuse? What does this imply about potential pitfalls in relying on existing statistics and how to handle those pitfalls?

4. Five years ago the ultraconservative newspaper (the only newspaper in your small, politically conservative city) published a scathing editorial attacking your agency for its efforts to help poor teenagers with unwanted pregnancies to secure abortions. The editorial urged elected officials to cut off your agency's public funding. Now, a social work doctoral student, for her dissertation, is conducting a historical/comparative analysis of possible changes in your agency's philosophy about abortion services, based on the content of the agency's annual reports and on letters written by the agency's executive directors. She tentatively concludes that the agency's philosophy has changed in the aftermath of the editorial, and that the agency now has become less supportive of the criticized abortion services. She shares her tentative conclusions with you because you are her friend and you have been a service provider at the agency for ten years. Based on your direct experience in providing services, you believe her conclusions are wrong. What would you advise her as to the risks inherent in relying on the accuracy of only one type of primary source, the reasons her sources may be biased and misleading, and additional sources she should obtain and analyze for corroborating evidence?

CHAPTER

Processing Data

OBJECTIVES

1. Describe how computers are being used as an aid in the delivery of social work services.
2. Provide a brief overview of the history of computers in social research.
3. Describe the difference between mainframe computers and microcomputers.
4. Identify the functions of coding.
5. Describe two different approaches to developing code categories, depending on your initial ability to anticipate responses.
6. Identify the attributes of good code categories.
7. Identify ways to assess coder errors.
8. Identify alternative data entry options.
9. Be able to construct a codebook.
10. Identify the functions of data cleaning and describe two ways to clean data codes.

PRACTICE-RELEVANT SUMMARY

As you may expect, this chapter is not the easiest one to relate to social work practice. Only recently have computers been recognized as useful in social work practice. And yet computers are becoming increasingly widespread throughout our society. Chances are you use one for word processing purposes in preparing your term papers. Of course, you may find that the word processing functions of computers are very helpful in your practice, such as when you need to write letters to clients, prepare group work agendas, send memos to colleagues, and so on.

But word processing is only the beginning. Computers can aid social work practitioners in many other ways. For example, if you work in an agency serving children, you may occasionally have to administer lengthy checklists to parents and teachers to assess whether children have attention deficit hyperactivity disorder or other internalized or externalized behavior problems. These checklists are complex and time consuming to score by hand. Fortunately, the agency can obtain software supplied by the checklist publishers that enables practitioners to obtain a child's scores in various problem areas in about ten minutes.

Computers enable social work administrators to have almost immediately at their fingertips a great deal of information about their agency's services and clientele, such as caseload trends, types of clients served and ways different clients may be being served differently, and so on. Public welfare social workers can use computers to guide case planning. Social workers in child welfare settings can use computer programs to guide child placement decisions. Case managers can use computers to track client activities and progress across a maze of service deliverers. Software has also been developed to help social workers evaluate their own practice via single-case evaluation techniques discussed in Chapter 10.

Software is also available to analyze data gathered across subjects in research using other types of designs and data collection methods. One commonly used program is denoted by the acronym *SPSS.* But there are many other programs, as well. Before the late 1970s the analysis of research data using these computer programs required using large computers, called *mainframes,* maintained in computer centers. Nowadays, fortunately, it is usually not necessary to share time with others and go to remote computer centers to obtain your data. This is because we now have *microcomputers,* also known as *personal computers,* that are capable of handling the same programs (like SPSS) and allowing you to conduct perhaps all of your analyses without leaving your office or agency.

Regardless of what type of computer you use, you will find that before you can conduct your analyses you must first *develop codes* that the computer can understand. There are two ways to develop codes. One involves using a coding scheme developed before analyzing your data. The second involves examining the data from a number of cases to determine the best categories to use in coding the data. Which approach to use depends on whether you are able, in advance, to anticipate all the responses likely to be relevant to your analysis. You will also need to develop a codebook, which describes the locations of variables and identifies the attributes of each variable and the code assigned to each attribute.

Various options exist for *entering your data* into your computer. Perhaps the most common method used by social workers is to precode your data collection instrument, so that data can be entered directly on your computer keyboard as you examine each completed data collection instrument. When you use this direct data entry method, it is essential that data collection instruments be edited carefully before data entry to check for problems in the way data were recorded on the instrument. An even more direct data entry method, resources permitting, is to have telephone interviewers record data directly into the computer while they are conducting their telephone interviews. Another expedient method is to use optical scanning sheets, in which a machine reads black pencil marks on special code sheets.

Regardless of which data entry method you use, and no matter how carefully your data have been entered, some errors are inevitable. Consequently, data entry should be followed by a *data cleaning* phase before any data analyses are conducted. There are two options for cleaning data: possible-code cleaning and contingency cleaning. Using *possible-code cleaning,* you examine the distribution of responses to each item in your data set and look to see if some responses exist for codes you didn't use (such as codes for categories other than male or female for a gender variable). Using *contingency cleaning,* you look for codes on one variable that coincide with codes on another variable that cannot possibly go together, such as when the same person is coded as a male and a mother, or when a couple is coded as not having any children but the age of their oldest child is recorded as nine.

REVIEW QUESTIONS

1. Social work practitioners can use computers to:
   a. Guide case planning
   b. Guide child placement decisions
   c. Track client activities in case management
   d. All of the above

2. Which of the following statements is true about the use of computers to process social work research data?
   a. It is necessary to use large, centralized mainframe computers.
   b. Software is available that enables data to be analyzed on personal computers (or microcomputers).
   c. Before you can analyze your data, you must know computer programming, so you can write your own computer program from scratch.
   d. None of the above.

3. Which of the following statements is true about coding?
   a. It is possible to develop a coding scheme before analyzing your data.
   b. One coding option involves examining the data from a number of cases to determine the best categories to use in coding the data.
   c. You will always be able to anticipate all the codes likely to be relevant to your analysis.
   d. All of the above.
   e. Only a and b are true.

4. A codebook should:
   a. Describe the locations of variables
   b. Identify the attributes of each variable
   c. Indicate the code assigned to each attribute
   d. All of the above

5. Which of the following statements is true about the use of the direct data entry method?

a. It is essential that data collection instruments be edited carefully before data entry to check for problems in the way data were recorded on the instrument.

b. You can assume that the data will be entered error free.

c. Data are transferred by means of edge coding from transfer sheets.

d. It cannot be done without using telephone surveys.

6. Which of the following statements is *not* true about data processing?

   a. Once data have been originally entered, you should assume that no incorrect data are in the data set.

   b. After data entry, data can be cleaned by examining distributions of responses and looking for responses with illegitimate codes.

   c. Data can be cleaned by looking for codes on one variable that coincide with other codes with which they should not coincide.

   d. Computers cannot be relied on to produce correct results if the data enetered into them are in error.

7–9: The following information was found in a codebook:

Column	Variable	Codes-Categories
1	Gender	1 = Female 2 = Male
2	Ethnicity	1 = White, not Hispanic 2 = White Hispanic 3 = Hispanic, not White 4 = African American 5 = Asian American 6 = Native American 7 = Other 9 = Not answered
3	Relationship to nursing home resident	1 = Husband 2 = Wife 3 = Son 4 = Daughter 5 = Other 9 = Not answered

7. Which of the following statements is true about a person with the following data entered in columns 1 through 3: 142?

   a. It is a female African American wife of a nursing home resident.

   b. It is the 142nd person in the data set.

c. It is a male African American husband of a nursing home resident.

d. It is a female Native American daughter of a nursing home resident.

8. Which of the following statements is true about a person with the following data entered in columns 1 through 3: 252?

   a. The person is male.

   b. The person is a resident's wife.

   c. The person is Native American.

   d. There is an error in the data entry.

9. Which of the following statements is true about a person with the following data entered in columns 1 through 3: 386?

   a. The person did not report their gender.

   b. Their ethnicity is "other."

   c. They have no relationship to the resident.

   d. There are errors in the data entry.

   e. All of the above.

EXERCISE 14.1

Develop a codebook for the following questionnaire:

1. Gender

☐ Female

☐ Male

2. Age: __ __

3. Student status in social work program:

☐ Undergraduate

☐ First-year master's degree student

☐ Second-year master's degree student

☐ Doctoral degree student

4. Satisfaction with social work education you have received so far at this program:

☐ Very satisfied

☐ Satisfied

☐ Dissatisfied

☐ Very dissatisfied

5. Have you ever read the Rubin and Babbie text, *Research Methods for Social Work*?

☐ Yes

☐ No

6. Did you enjoy reading the Rubin and Babbie text, *Research Methods for Social Work*?

☐ Yes

☐ No

☐ Not applicable, I didn't read it

EXERCISE 14.2

1. Describe two different approaches for determining whether incorrect data were entered for items 5 and/or 6 of the above questionnaire. Indicate codes to either or both items that would imply an error(s) in data entry.

2. How would you go about correcting the data?

DISCUSSION QUESTIONS

1. Describe at least two ways a computer can be useful to you in your social work practice.

2. What does the phrase "garbage in, garbage out" mean to you with respect to data entry and data cleaning?

3. Describe how you would go about cleaning your data using possible-code cleaning. Describe how you would do it using contingency cleaning.

CHAPTER

Interpreting Descriptive Statistics and Tables

OBJECTIVES

1. Interpret a univariate distribution of data.
2. Calculate and interpret the three measures of central tendency.
3. Understand and interpret the role of measures of dispersion.
4. Calculate and interpret standard deviation.
5. Differentiate continuous and discrete variables, and select the appropriate calculation for each.
6. Construct and interpret collapsed response categories.
7. Construct and interpret tables that make bivariate subgroup comparisons.
8. Construct and interpret multivariate tables.
9. Recognize the potential influence that suppressor, distorter, and antecedent variables can have on bivariate findings.
10. Illustrate a spurious relationship in social work practice research.
11. Recognize how the inclusion of qualitative findings can enhance the interpretation of descriptive statistics and how the inclusion of descriptive statistics can enrich a qualitative study.

PRACTICE-RELEVANT SUMMARY

No matter how much you may dislike or fear statistics, there is no escaping them. You may encounter them less as a direct practitioner of social work than as an accountant, but encounter them you will, and this chapter will help you deal with them when you must.

Some day, for example, you may be asked to present data summarizing the characteristics of clients in your unit or agency. If the purpose of the report is solely descriptive, chances are you will undertake a univariate analysis, which examines one variable at a time (in contrast to bivariate analysis, which examines two variables in relation to one another). To make your presentation manageable, you will probably construct a frequency distribution, which reports the number and percentage of cases in each attribute of each variable. To make your presentation even more manageable, you might collapse response categories of attributes into grouped categories of attributes, called *marginals*, and then report the raw numbers and the percentages of the marginals.

To further summarize the data, you would present measures of central tendency and dispersion. If you have *continuous variables* (variables at the interval or ratio level of measurement), you could present all three *measures of central tendency:* the mean, the median, and the mode. The *mean* is calculated by summing the values and then dividing the sum by the number of cases. The *median* is the middle value in the distribution. The *mode* is the most frequent value. If you have *discrete variables* (variables at the nominal or ordinal level of measurement), you would be restricted to the mode unless you violated some technical assumptions (which is often done).

Measures of central tendency don't give the whole picture, however. An average age of 45, for example, could come from an agency where half the cases are 10 years old and the other half are 80 years old. To depict how spread out the values are, you can present *measures of dispersion*. The range shows the distance separating the highest from the lowest value. The *interquartile range* is the range of scores for the middle 50% of cases. The *standard deviation* gives a sense of how far each case, on average, is from the mean. In a normal curve (a bell curve), 68% of the cases fall between one standard deviation above and below the mean. The standard deviation is calculated by subtracting the mean from each score, squaring the difference, summing the squares, dividing the sum of squares by the number of cases, and then finding the square root of the dividend.

Perhaps your report will need to go beyond describing each variable one at a time. Perhaps you will need to make subgroup comparisons across more than one variable. In a *bivariate analysis,* you will compare the subgroup values of one variable to the subgroup values of a second variable. For example, perhaps your funding source wants to know whether the degree of satisfaction expressed by ethnic minority clients is as high as the degree of satisfaction expressed by white clients.

In constructing a *bivariate table,* typically you will put the categories of the independent variable in the columns and the categories of the dependent variable in the rows. Then you will calculate and present the percentages of the categories of the columns. In reading a bivariate table constucted in this manner, you will compare the percentages across each row. Thus, column 1 might show that 75% of whites are satisfied and 25% are dissatisfied, and column 2 might show that 60% of minorities are satisfied and 40% are dissatisfied. Some bivariate tables deviate from convention, presenting the independent variable categories in the rows and the dependent variable categories in the columns. This is okay, as long as the percentages are now presented in the rows. The percentages should be calculated and presented according to the independent variable, regardless of whether it appears in the columns (as is customary) or the rows.

Additional guidelines for bivariate table construction include the following: (1) a table title should succinctly describe its contents; (2) the original content of the variables should be clearly presented; (3) the attributes of each variable should be clearly indicated; (4) the base on which percentages are calculated should be indicated; and (5) if any cases are omitted from the table because of missing data, their numbers should be indicated.

Your report may need to examine more than two variables simultaneously. This would require a *multivariate analysis.* For example, you may have to examine client satisfaction in relation to both gender and ethnicity simultaneously. Thus, you would compare the satisfaction of minority males, minority females, white males, and white females. The construction and interpretation of *multivariate tables* follows essentially the same steps that apply to bivariate tables. One way to simplify the interpretation of a multivariate table is by visually imagining it as two or more bivariate tables. Then interpret each bivariate table separately for each category of the third variable.

Some multivariate analyses help us elaborate on a bivariate relationship, in what is called the *elaboration model.* If the original bivariate relationship remains essentially unchanged for each category of additional variables introduced in the analysis, we can say that the original relationship has been replicated. If the original relationship disappears when additional variables are introduced in the analysis, the original relationship can be explained away as spurious. Sometimes the introduction of additional variables strengthens the original relationship. If so, the additional variables are called *suppressor variables,* because before they were controlled, they were suppressing the true strength of the relationship. Sometimes two variables that were positively related in a bivariate analysis become negatively related when additional variables are introduced. When this happens, the additional variables are called *distorter variables.*

Conducting a qualitative inquiry can enhance the interpretation of descriptive statistics by providing insights into their potential meanings. Likewise, the inclusion of descriptive statistics can enrich a qualitative study, since counting some things is an inescapable part of detecting patterns or developing a deeper understanding of the phenomenon being studied.

REVIEW QUESTIONS

1–6: Below are the ages of the nine children on your caseload at a child guidance center:

3 3 3 3 4 8 9 10 11

1. 6 is the

   a. Mean c. Mode

   b. Median d. Range

2. 4 is the

   a. Mean c. Mode

   b. Median d. Range

3. 3 is the

   a. Mean c. Mode

   b. Median d. Range

4. 8 is the
   a. Mean
   b. Median
   c. Mode
   d. Range

5. The square root of 10.4 is the
   a. Mean
   b. Median
   c. Standard deviation
   d. Interquartile range

6. Which of the following statements is true about the above distribution of ages?
   a. It is from a continuous variable.
   b. It is from a discrete variable.
   c. It contains no dispersion.
   d. The data are grouped into collapsed response categories.
   e. All of the above.

7–8: Below is a table showing the number of clients on medication and not on medication for male and female child therapists:

	Male Therapists	Female Therapists
Number on medication	40	40
Number not on medication	60	160

7. Which of the following statements is true about the table?
   a. There is no relationship between gender of therapist and likelihood that client is on medication.
   b. The clients of male therapists are more likely to be on medication.
   c. The clients of female therapists are more likely to be on medication.
   d. It is a multivariate table.
   e. a and d, only, are true.

8. Which of the following statements is true about the table?
   a. It should be percentaged according to the column variable.
   b. It should be percentaged according to the row variable.
   c. It does not matter whether it is percentaged by row or column.

d. It is a univariate table.

e. Only c and d are true.

9–11: Below is a table showing the number of clients on medication and not on medication for male and female child therapists, controlling for whether the child has attention deficit hyperactivity disorder (ADHD):

	Clients with ADHD		Non-ADHD Clients	
	MALE THERAPISTS	FEMALE THERAPISTS	MALE THERAPISTS	FEMALE THERAPISTS
Number on medication	30	13	10	27
Number not on medication	0	0	60	160

9. Which of the following statements is true about the table?
   a. There is no relationship between gender of therapist and likelihood that client is on medication.
   b. The clients of male therapists are more likely to be on medication.
   c. The clients of female therapists are more likely to be on medication.
   d. It is a bivariate table.
   e. Only b and d are true.
   f. Only c and d are true.

10. Which of the following statements is true about the table?
    a. Children with ADHD are more likely to be on medication.
    b. Children with ADHD are more likely to have male therapists.
    c. Gender of therapist is the independent variable.
    d. All of the above.
    e. None of the above.

11. If the above table is based on the same clients that were in the table for items 7 and 8, which of the following statements is true about both tables taken as a whole?
    a. The original relationship was replicated.
    b. The original relationship was spurious.

c. Whether the child has ADHD is a supressor variable.

d. Whether the child has ADHD is a distorter variable.

EXERCISE 15.1

The number of timeouts during the 10 sessions of play therapy for each of the 20 children in your play therapy groups is listed below:

0	16	20	4	0
3	17	18	0	1
0	5	2	1	0
3	2	3	0	5

1. Construct a univariate frequency distribution with grouped data in four collapsed response categories, showing the percentages for each collapsed category.

2. Calculate the mean and state what it indicates.

3. Calculate the median and state what it indicates.

4. Calculate the mode and state what it indicates.

5. Discuss the advantages and disadvantages of the above three measures of central tendency you have calculated in terms of how well they summarize the distribution.

6. Calculate the range and state what it indicates.

7. Calculate the standard deviation and interpret it.

EXERCISE 15.2

Below is a hypothetical table showing the number of students in a high-risk neighborhood who graduated and dropped out of high school. Also indicated is whether they received the services of a social worker and whether their socioeconomic status (SES) was below the poverty line.

Received Social Services?	SES Below Poverty Line?	Dropped Out?	Frequency
Yes	Below	Yes	400
Yes	Below	No	400
Yes	Above	Yes	50
Yes	Above	No	150
No	Below	Yes	250
No	Below	No	50
No	Above	Yes	100
No	Above	No	200

1. Construct and interpret a bivariate table for examining the relationship between receiving social work services and dropping out of high school. (*Tip:* Be sure to percentage the table appropriately.)

2. Construct and interpret a bivariate table for examining the relationship between SES and dropping out of high school. (*Tip:* Be sure to percentage the table appropriately.)

3. Construct and interpret a bivariate table for examining the relationship between receiving social work services and SES. (*Tip:* Be sure to percentage the table appropriately.)

4. Construct and interpret a multivariate table for examining the relationship between receiving social work services and dropping out of high school, after controlling for SES. (*Tip:* Be sure to percentage the table appropriately.)

5. Explain why the bivariate relationship between receiving social work services and dropping out of high school did or did not change after controlling for SES.

6. In light of your answers to numbers 4 and 5, what kind of elaboration model variable was SES? Explain.

DISCUSSION QUESTIONS

1. Explain the role of percentages in bivariate and multivariate tables and the importance of percentaging in the right direction.

2. Why is it important to report both the mean and the median? Why won't reporting just one suffice?

3. Provide hypothetical examples of multivariate relationships relevant to social work practice that illustrate each of the following:

a. A spurious relationship

b. A suppressor variable

c. A distorter variable

4. Provide a hypothetical example of how combining descriptive statistics with a qualitative inquiry can enrich the qualitative inquiry as well as the interpretation of the descriptive statistics.

CHAPTER

Inferential Data Analysis: Part 1

OBJECTIVES

1. Explain the role of chance as a possible explanation for some observed correlations between variables in a sample.
2. Explain the role of statistical significance testing as a basis for refuting chance.
3. Discuss the role of theoretical sampling distributions in the concept of statistical significance.
4. Define statistical significance.
5. Discuss the criteria for selecting a significance level.
6. Define the critical region in a theoretical sampling distribution.
7. Define and identify when to use one- and two-tailed tests of significance.
8. Discuss the role of the null hypothesis and how it compares to the research hypothesis.
9. Define Type I and Type II errors and discuss the importance of each in social work research.
10. Discuss the impact of sample size on statistical significance, and how that bears on assessing relationship magnitude and considering substantive significance.
11. Interpret measures of association and their role in inferential data analysis.
12. Calculate and interpret the *z*-score approach to effect size.
13. Explain how the concepts of statistical significance, relationship magnitude (or effect size), and substantive significance are different, and how each gets considered as part of interpreting inferential data.
14. Discuss the bases for considering whether effect sizes are strong, medium, or weak, and the influence of value judgments on variations across studies in the substantive significance of the same effect size.

PRACTICE-RELEVANT SUMMARY

Just as there is no escaping descriptive statistics, there is no escaping inferential statistics—at least not if you ever want your practice to be guided by your utilization of research that tests hypotheses relevant to social work.

Beyond *utilizing* research, someday you are likely to be asked to present data indicating the impact your unit or agency is having on some desired aim. Some of the folks asking for such data are likely to know about inferential statistics and the role chance might play in accounting for outcomes that on the surface might seem to suggest that your unit or agency is successfully achieving its aims. If and when you are faced with this situation, your practice will be more effective (that is, you will be better equipped to present your unit's or agency's data in an informed, persuasive manner) if you are able to include inferential data analysis procedures in your report—procedures that will inform your audience of the likelihood that chance (or sampling error) accounts for your findings. These procedures will also give your audience hard data indicating the strength of your unit's or agency's impact, data that can be used as a basis for discussing the ultimate value (that is, the substantive significance) of the impact you are having.

The first step in the inferential data analysis process is to ascertain the probability that chance, or sampling error, accounts for your findings. In any study of any independent and dependent variables, even when there is no relationship in the population between those variables, there is a good chance of obtaining findings that show some relationship between those variables in your sample, although that relationship might be quite weak. The process of assessing the probability that chance explains your findings involves testing to see if the relationship you have observed is statistically significant. *Testing for statistical significance* means calculating the probability, or odds, of finding due to chance a relationship at least as strong as the one you have observed in your findings.

All of the methods for calculating statistical significance, no matter how different their mathematical assumptions and formulas may be, ultimately yield the same thing—a probability between 0 and 1.0 that the observed relationship was obtained simply due to chance. Tests of statistical significance ascertain that probability by using theoretical sampling distributions. *Theoretical sampling distributions* show what proportion of random distributions of data would produce relationships at least as strong as the one observed in your findings. The theoretical sampling distribution thus shows the probability that observing the relationship you observed was due to the luck of the draw when and if no such relationship really exists in a population or in a theoretical sense.

The probability that the observed relationship could have been produced by chance is compared to a preselected level of significance. If that probability is equal to or less than that level of significance, the finding is deemed statistically significant and the plausibility of the null hypothesis (chance) is refuted.

Traditionally, social scientists, including social work researchers, have settled on .05 as the most commonly used cutoff point to separate findings not deemed significant from those that are. However, a higher or lower level can be justified depending on the research context. Findings that fall in the zone beyond the cutoff point, and that are therefore considered statistically significant, comprise the critical region of the theoretical sampling distribution. The cutoff point is called the *level of significance*. When it is set at .05, it is signified by the following expression: $p \leq .05$. This means that any probability equal to or less than .05 will be deemed statistically significant. Researchers usually just report it as less than .05 ($p < .05$) because the probability rarely equals .05 exactly. A probability that is even a tiny bit above .05 would be considered to be greater than .05—outside of the critical region—and therefore statistically not significant.

Hypotheses that do not specify whether the predicted relationship will be positive or negative are called *nondirectional hypotheses.* When testing nondirectional hypotheses, we must use two-tailed tests of significance. *Two-tailed tests of significance* place the critical regions at both ends of the theoretical sampling distribution. When testing directional hypotheses we can use *one-tailed tests of significance.* These locate the critical region of significant values at one, predicted end of the theoretical sampling distribution.

When we refer to chance as a rival hypothesis, we call it the null hypothesis. The *null hypothesis* postulates that the relationship being statistically tested is explained by chance—that it does not really exist in a population or in a theoretical sense—even though it may seem to be related in our particular findings. Thus, when our findings are shown to be statistically significant, we reject the null hypothesis because the probability that it is true—that our results were caused by chance—is less than our level of significance. Whenever we reject the null hypothesis, we are supporting the plausibility of our research hypothesis (assuming that we are predicting that two variables are related and that we are not seeking to show that they are unrelated). Conversely, whenever we fail to reject the null hypothesis, we are failing to support our research hypothesis.

Every time we make a decision about the statistical significance of a tested relationship, we risk making an error. If we decide to reject the null hypothesis, we risk making one type of error. If we do not reject the null hypothesis, we risk making another type of error. *Type I errors* occur when we reject a true null hypothesis. *Type II errors* occur when we accept a false null hypothesis. Social scientists tend to accept a much lower risk of making a Type I error than a Type II error. But just because so many social scientists conform to this convention does not mean that Type I errors are necessarily more serious than Type II errors, especially when human suffering is at stake. Deciding which type of error is more serious requires making value judgments, and the choice will vary depending on the nature and context of the research question.

The larger our sample, the less sampling error we have. Therefore, increasing sample size reduces the risk of a Type II error. However, with very large samples, weak and not particularly meaningful relationships can become statistically significant. When we assess statistical significance, we ask only one question: "Can a relationship be inferred to exist in a theoretical sense or in a broader population?" We do not assess how strong the relationship is. Significance levels do *not* indicate the relative strength of a relationship. A relationship significant at the .001 level is not necessarily stronger than one significant at the .05 level. A weak relationship can be significant at the .001 level if the sample size is very large, and a stronger relationship might be significant at the .05 level but not at a lower level if the sample size is not large.

Measures of association, such as correlation coefficients and analogous statistics (phi, rho, Cramer's V, gamma, eta, and so on), assess how strong a relationship is. Which measure of association should be used depends primarily on the level of measurement of your variables. The stronger the relationship, the closer the measure-of-association statistic will be to 1.0 or –1.0. The weaker the relationship, the closer it will be to zero. Many measures of association are based on a *proportionate-reduction-of-error* (PRE) model and tell us how much error in predicting attributes of a dependent variable is reduced by knowledge of the attribute of the independent variable.

Many measure-of-association statistics can be squared to indicate the proportion of variation in the dependent variable that is explained by one or more independent variables.

Statistics that portray the strength of association between variables are often referred to by the term *effect size*. This term is particularly common in clinical outcome research. Effect-size statistics might refer to proportion of dependent variable variation explained or to the difference between the means of two groups divided by the standard deviation (that is, the *z*-score). Effect-size statistics portray the strength of association found in any study, no matter what outcome measure is used, in terms that are comparable across studies. Thus, they enable us to compare the effects of different interventions across studies using different types of outcome measures. *Z-score effect sizes* of about .5 to .7 are generally considered to be medium or average in strength. These correspond to correlations of roughly about .30, give or take several points. Larger effect sizes are considered strong, and effect sizes well below .4 (correlations near about .1) are generally considered to be weak.

Statistical significance, relationship strength, and *substantive significance* must not be confused with one another. Statistically significant relationships are not necessarily strong or substantively meaningful. Strong relationships are not necessarily substantively significant, and some seemingly weak relationships can have great substantive significance. The substantive significance of a finding pertains to its practical or theoretical value or meaningfulness; it cannot be assessed without making value judgments about the importance of the variables or problem studied, what the finding adds to what is already known or not known about alleviating a problem, whether the benefits of implementing the study's implications are worth the costs of that implementation, and so on.

REVIEW QUESTIONS

1. In trying to understand why many clients prematurely terminate services in your agency, you find that 51% of males terminate, compared to 49% of females. Which of the following statements is true about the process of inferential data analysis regarding this finding?

   a. You should ascertain the probability that chance, or sampling error, accounts for the difference between the men and women.

   b. You should infer that men are more likely to prematurely terminate than are women.

   c. You should infer that a relationship exists between gender and premature termination.

   d. Both b and c, only, are true.

2. Which of the following statements is true about testing for statistical significance?

   a. Even weak relationships can be statistically significant.

   b. It involves assessing the probability that chance explains our findings.

c. It will yield a probability between 0 and 1.0 that the observed relationship was obtained simply due to chance.

d. All of the above.

e. None of the above.

3. Which of the following statements is true about theoretical sampling distributions?

a. They show what proportion of random distributions of data would produce relationships at least as strong as the one observed in our findings.

b. They show the probability that observing the relationship we observed was due to the luck of the draw when and if no such relationship really exists in a population or in a theoretical sense.

c. The critical region of the distribution is preselected.

d. All of the above.

e. None of the above.

4. The .05 level of significance is commonly chosen because:

a. Mathematics dictates it as the only correct level.

b. It means there is at least a .05 correlation between the independent and dependent variables.

c. Two groups would have to show a .05 difference in order to be significant.

d. All of the above.

e. None of the above.

5. Refuting the null hypothesis means:

a. Rejecting the research hypothesis

b. Refuting chance as a plausible explanation for the findings

c. Not having statistically significant results

d. Proving that the research hypothesis is true

6. One-tailed tests of significance can be used when:

a. We test hypotheses that do not specify whether the predicted relationship will be positive or negative.

b. We test nondirectional hypotheses.

c. We test directional hypotheses.

d. We split the critical region of significant values at both ends of the theoretical sampling distribution.

7. Which of the following statements is true about Type I and Type II errors?

a. Every time we make a decision about the statistical significance of a tested relationship, we risk making either a Type I or a Type II error.
b. Type I errors are always more serious than Type II errors.
c. Type I errors occur when we accept a false null hypothesis.
d. Type II errors occur when we reject a true null hypothesis.
e. All of the above.

8. Larger samples:
   a. Have less sampling error
   b. Have less risk of a Type II error
   c Are more likely to find that weak relationships are statistically significant
   d. All of the above

9. Which of the following statements is true about significance levels?
   a. They indicate how strong the relationship is.
   b. A relationship significant at the .001 level is stronger than one significant at the .05 level.
   c. A weak relationship can be significant at the .001 level if the sample size is very large.
   d. A strong relationship will always be significant at the .05 level, regardless of sample size.

10. Which of the following statements is true about measures of association?
    a. They assess how strong a relationship is.
    b. Which measure of association to use depends primarily on the level of measurement of your variables.
    c. Some measures of association range between 0 and 1.
    d. Many measure-of-association statistics can be squared to indicate the proportion of variation in the dependent variable that is explained by the independent variables.
    e. All of the above.

11. In an evaluation of the effectiveness of an intervention to reduce depression, the experimental group's posttest mean is 20, which indicates less depression than the control group's posttest mean of 30. The standard deviation is 5. The effect size is:

    a. + 2
    b. + 10
    c. – 2
    d. – 10

12. Which of the following statements is true about effect size statistics?
    a. They show whether the finding is statistically significant.
    b. They show whether the finding is substantively significant.
    c. They enable us to compare the effects of different interventions across studies using different types of outcome measures.
    d. If they fall below .30, they are not significant.
    e. All of the above.
    f. Only a and d are true.

13. Which of the following statements is true about substantive significance?
    a. Strong relationships will be substantively significant.
    b. It is possible for a weak relationship to be substantively significant.
    c. Assessing the substantive significance of a finding requires that we avoid making value judgments.
    d. All of the above.

14. Suppose you evaluate the effectiveness of your agency's program and find that program recipients had better outcomes than nonrecipients, but the results are not statistically significant. This means that:
    a. The program was not effective.
    b. The program was effective, but not at a significant level.
    c. Sampling error cannot be ruled out as an explanation for the difference in outcomes.
    d. None of the above.

EXERCISE 16.1

A program evaluation study with an extremely rigorous experimental design assesses the effectiveness of a program to prevent child abuse among high-risk families by providing them with intensive, comprehensive social work services. Using a valid measurement of actual abuse, it finds that the experimental group families had a mean of .1 incidents of abuse, compared to a control group mean of .3. The standard deviation was .4. The significance level was .05, and the probability of committing a Type I error was less than .05.

1. Were the results statistically significant? Specify the basis for your answer.

2. What type of error would you be choosing to risk, given your answer to the previous questions?

3. Should a one- or two-tailed test of significance have been used? Why?

4. What was the effect size? Was it positive or negative, and why? Would you consider it to be strong, medium, or weak, and why?

5. Discuss whether you would find these results substantively significant, and why.

EXERCISE 16.2

Another program evaluation study with a moderately rigorous quasi-experimental design assesses the effectiveness of a parent education program to improve knowledge of child-rearing among parents at high risk for child abuse by providing them with ten sessions of parent education classes. Using a self-report scale that the program evaluators constructed for the purpose of this evaluation, the study finds that the parents who participated in the classes had a mean score of 50, which was better than the comparison group's mean score of 30, indicating that the program recipients provided more correct answers about child-rearing. The standard deviation was 10. The significance level was .05, and the probability of committing a Type I error was less than .001.

1. Were the results statistically significant? Specify the basis for your answer.

2. What type of error would you be choosing to risk, given your answer to the previous question?

3. Should a one- or two-tailed test of significance have been used? Why?

4. What was the effect size? Was it positive or negative, and why? Would you consider it to be strong, medium, or weak, and why?

5. Discuss whether you would find these results substantively significant, and why.

EXERCISE 16.3

A third program evaluation study with a moderately rigorous quasi-experimental design assesses the effectiveness of a family preservation program whose aim is to prevent the out-of-home placement of children of parents who have been referred by the courts for child abuse or neglect. The program measures its outcome not in terms of actual child abuse, but simply according to whether or not children are placed out of the home. It finds that only 10% of the children in the families receiving family preservation services were placed out of the home, compared to 50% of children in a comparison group receiving routine child welfare services. The strength of this relationship, measured by the phi statistic, was .30, which becomes .09 when squared. The significance level was .05, and the probability of committing a Type I error was less than .01.

1. Were the results statistically significant? Specify the basis for your answer.

2. What type of error would you be choosing to risk, given your answer to the previous question?

3. Would you consider the phi statistic of .30 to indicate a strong, medium, or weak relationship, and why?

4. What does the phi-squared of .09 mean?

5. Discuss whether you would find these results substantively significant, and why.

EXERCISE 16.4

1. Reexamine each of the above three program evaluation vignettes in Exercises 16.1 to 16.3. Considering the findings as well as design issues and the nature of the outcome variables measured, which of the three outcomes would you consider most and least substantively significant? Why?

2. Suppose you had relatively meager funding to develop a program either for preventing child abuse or for intervening with parents referred for child abuse. Suppose that the target population for your program was very large, and that the parent education approach would reach ten times as many high-risk families as would either of the other two approaches (in Exercises 16.1 and 16.3). In light of this consideration, as well as your answer to question 1 above, which of the three program approaches would you develop in your program (assuming that you could afford to choose only one, that you decided to be guided by research in your decision, and that these three studies represented the research)? Discuss the reasons for your selection.

DISCUSSION QUESTIONS

1. Suppose an evaluation of a program to prevent teen pregnancy is conducted with a very small sample. It finds that none of the ten teens in the experimental group became pregnant, while two of the ten teens in the control group became pregnant. However, the results are not statistically significant. Discuss how you would interpret these results, keeping in mind issues of Type II errors and the influence of sample size. What would you recommend be done by the field in light of these results?

2. Discuss the purpose of the null hypothesis. Why do we need one? In your answer, discuss why/how both the null hypothesis and the research hypothesis can be false.

3. Suppose you conducted an evaluation of a spouse abuse treatment program with a ridiculously small sample size of only two men in the experimental group and two men in the control group. Construct a theoretical sampling distribution, as follows. Give each man a fake name, and then divide the names into all possible dichotomous outcome arrangements of names (that is, all four commit further abuse, none do, three do and one doesn't, and so on). After you exhaust all possible outcomes, you should have 16 different arrangements of names. The probability of each possible arrangement (or outcome) is 1/16, or .0625. Would it be possible for this study to come up with statistically significant findings with a .05 significance level? Why or why not? Discuss what this illustrates about the influence of sample size on statistical significance and the risk of Type II errors.

4. When they learn that judging the substantive significance of a finding involves making value judgments, some students conclude that the whole business of inferential statistics is irrelevant—that in the end everything is completely subjective. Do you agree with them? Why or why not? If you disagree with them, indicate the ways science and objectivity play a big role in the process, despite the inescapable involvement of some value judgments.

CHAPTER

Inferential Data Analysis: Part 2

OBJECTIVES

1. Define statistical power.
2. Incorporate statistical power considerations in utilizing research with null findings to guide practice.
3. Explain the role of statistical power analysis in planning research studies or in interpreting the implications of the results of these studies for practice.
4. Identify the risks inherent in neglecting statistical power considerations in planning or utilizing research.
5. Utilize meta-analyses as a basis for selecting a priori effect sizes in statistical power analysis in planning research.
6. Utilize meta-analyses as a guide to practice.
7. Identify the pitfalls inherent in meta-analysis methods.
8. Select tests of statistical significance that fit the relevant methodological characteristics of a study.
9. Identify the criteria for using parametric versus nonparametric tests of statistical significance and the differences between them.
10. Understand and apply to practice the results of studies reporting multivariate analyses.
11. Identify and discuss common misuses and misinterpretations of inferential statistics.
12. Identify and discuss common controversies in the use of inferential statistics.

PRACTICE-RELEVANT SUMMARY

The summary of Chapter 16 began by asserting that there is no way to escape inferential statistics in utilizing hypothesis testing research to guide your practice. Chapter 17 continues the discussion of inferential data analysis begun in Chapter 16, but in connection to some statistical concepts that you will probably experience as more advanced and more challenging than most of the material in the previous chapter.

The first concept to be considered, statistical power analysis, actually is extremely relevant to social work practice. It is terribly important that practitioners be able to understand and apply statistical power analysis, even if they only utilize research to guide their practice, and never do research. The basis for this assertion is that many practice evaluation studies report findings that fall short of statistical significance and therefore fail to confirm hypotheses about practice effectiveness. Thus, they risk making Type II errors.

Statistical power analysis enables us to calculate the risk of making a Type II error when we fail to support hypotheses about the effectiveness of a particular intervention or program. Thus, even if we are only utilizing the research of others about practice or program effectiveness and not conducting the research ourselves, it is essential that we perform a statistical power analysis on the study we are utilizing, so we will know the likelihood that the study has made a Type II error in failing to support the effectiveness of the intervention or program we are considering for our own use. If we find that that likelihood is high, we might want to still consider utilizing the tested intervention or program, despite the study's failure to reject the null hypothesis. If, on the other hand, we find that the likelihood of a Type II error is tiny, we might put much more stock in the lack of statistical significance in the findings and be persuaded not to adopt the tested intervention or program for our own use.

We can conduct statistical power analyses, and thus estimate the probability of committing Type II errors, simply by examining statistical power tables like Table 17-1, which displays the power of testing the significance of correlation coefficients at the .05 and .10 levels of significance for small, medium, and large effect sizes. In using Table 17-1 to plan a research study, the first step is to choose a significance level. The next step is to estimate the strength of the correlation between your independent and dependent variables that you expect exists in the population. The columns in the table pertain to small, medium, and large effect sizes. The figures in the columns indicate the probability of correctly rejecting the null hypothesis at different levels of sample size. Therefore, the probability of incorrectly rejecting the null hypothesis—which is the probability of committing a Type II error—is 1.00 minus the figure in the column. The figure in the column is the statistical power, and subtracting the power from 1.00 gives you the probability of committing a Type II error.

By using Table 17-1, you can select a sample size that will provide you with the level of risk of a Type II error that you desire. You can also use Table 17-1 to calculate the probability that studies you are reading have committed a Type II error. To do this, you follow the same steps as above, but simply use the correlation and sample size already reported in the study to locate the study's power.

Another advanced statistical concept connected to statistical power analysis and highly relevant to social work practice is meta-analysis. *Meta-analyses* help us select an appropriate a priori correlation when conducting a statistical power analysis in the planning of a research study. Meta-analyses also help us in attempting to develop practice guidelines from studies with diverse findings about the same research questions about practice. Meta-analysis involves calculating the mean effect size across previously completed research studies on a particular topic.

In addition, more complex meta-analytic procedures can be used to calculate the statistical significance of an overall set of results aggregated across various studies. The results of meta-analyses give us benchmarks for considering the relative effectiveness of various interventions. A related benefit of meta-analysis is its ability to ascertain how the mean effect size varies depending on various clinical or methodological factors.

Despite its benefits, meta-analysis has limitations and is controversial. Poorly conducted meta-analyses might lump together studies that are methodologically strong with those that have serious methodological limitations and treat their results equally in the analysis. The results of meta-analyses done this way can be misleading because the findings of methodologically strong studies should outweigh dubious findings produced by methodologically weak studies. Some meta-analysts have rated the methodological quality of studies and then used that rating as a factor in their meta-analyses. The reliability and validity of those ratings, however, is open to question. Some meta-analysts simply exclude studies with poor methodologies. However, there is no guarantee that their methodological judgment will be adequate in this regard. Another potential pitfall in meta-analysis involves sampling bias, which can result when the meta-analyst misses some important studies or when research with null outcomes is not published.

One topic in Chapter 17 that is harder to relate to practice involves the criteria for selecting the proper test of statistical significance. Nevertheless, it is important that practitioners be familiar with these criteria, so they are not entirely mystified when interacting with researchers or program evaluators or when reading their reports. The prime criteria influencing the selection of a statistical significance test are: (1) the level of measurement of the variables, (2) the number of variables included in the analysis (bivariate or multivariate) and the number of categories in the nominal variables, (3) the type of sampling methods used in data collection, and (4) the way the variables are distributed in the population to which the study seeks to generalize. Depending on a study's attributes regarding these criteria, a selection will be made between two broad types of significance tests: parametric tests and nonparametric tests. *Parametric tests* assume that at least one of the variables being studied has an interval or ratio level of measurement, that the sampling distribution of the relevant parameters of those variables is normal, and that the different groups being compared have been randomly selected and are independent of one another. Commonly used parametric tests include the *t*-test, analysis of variance, and Pearson product-moment correlation. *Nonparametric tests,* on the other hand, have been created for use when not all of the assumptions of parametric statistics can be met. Most can be used with nominal- or ordinal-level data that are not distributed normally. Some do not require independently selected samples.

The most commonly used nonparametric test is *chi-square,* which is used when we are treating both our independent and dependent variables as nominal-level. The chi-square test assesses the extent to which the frequencies you observe in your table of results differ from what you would expect to observe if the distribution was created by chance.

Commonly used parametric tests include the *t*-test, analysis of variance (ANOVA), and Pearson product-moment correlation (*r*). The *t-test* is appropriate for use with a dichotomous nominal independent variable and an interval- or ratio-level dependent variable. *ANOVA* can be used to test for the significance of bivariate and multivariate relationships. Like *t*-tests, the dependent variable must be interval- or ratio-level. When testing bivariate relationships, the only difference between ANOVA and the *t*-test is that the *t*-test can be applied only when the independent variable is dichotomous. ANOVA, on the other hand, can be used when the independent variable has more than two categories. The *Pearson product-moment correlation* (r) is used when both the independent and dependent variables are at the interval or ratio level of measurement. It can be used both as a measure of association and to test for statistical significance.

Inferential statistical tests can be used at the bivariate or multivariate level of data analysis. Partial correlation coefficients, for example, have the same meaning and uses as do bivariate correlations except that they measure the association between two variables after other, extraneous variables have been controlled. A commonly used extension of correlational analysis for multivariate inferences is multiple regression analysis. *Multiple regression analysis* shows the overall correlation between each of a set of independent variables and an interval- or ratio-level dependent variable. A multivariate statistic analogous to multiple regression analysis, but designed for use when the dependent variable is dichotomous, is called *discriminant function analysis.*

Inferential statistics are commonly misused and misinterpreted by the producers and consumers of social research. These errors are common across social science disciplines, not just in social work research. Common mistakes include the failure to consider statistical power, the belief that failure to reject the null hypothesis means the same thing as verifying it, interpreting a rejection of the null hypothesis as a confirmation of the research hypothesis, failing to distinguish between statistical significance and relationship strength, failing to distinguish substantive significance from either statistical significance or relationship strength, and conducting multiple bivariate tests of significance without adjusting for the inflated probability of committing a Type I error.

There are some basic issues in the use of inferential statistics about which even the foremost authorities on statistics disagree. One point of disagreement concerns whether statistical significance is irrelevant and misleading unless all of the assumptions of the chosen significance test have been met. Some statisticians prefer parametric tests of significance over nonparametric tests even when the characteristics of the variables being tested call for the use of nonparametric tests. Statisticians also disagree as to whether tests of significance can be applied to data gathered from an entire population rather than a sample. The best statistical options are often debatable. When analyzing your own data you should use whatever procedure you judge to be best in light of what you have learned and not to let these controversies immobilize you. Also, when you encounter research done by others that seems to be methodologically rigorous, you should not disregard it just because its inferential statistics violate some assumptions. The replication process ultimately should be used to verify the generalizations made in any particular study.

REVIEW QUESTIONS

1. When we conduct a statistical power analysis, we:
   a. Calculate the probability of avoiding a Type II error.
   b. Subtract from one the probability of making a Type II error.

c. Calculate the odds that our results were due to chance.

d. All of the above.

e. None of the above.

f. Only a and b are correct.

2. Conducting a statistical power analysis in planning a study will help us:

   a. Identify a desired sample size

   b. Pick an appropriate significance level

   c. Know the likelihood of obtaining findings that would support a true hypothesis

   d. All of the above

   e. None of the above

   f. Only a and b are correct

3. We can increase statistical power by:

   a. Increasing sample size

   b. Using a lower (more stringent) significance level

   c. Assuming a weaker relationship in the population

   d. All of the above

   e. None of the above

   f. Only b and c are correct

4. Which of the following statements is true about considering the statistical power of a completed study?

   a. Statistical power is no longer relevant, since the study has already been completed.

   b. The study's reported findings can be used for the correlation column in a statistical power table.

   c. Subtract the significance level from 1.0 to find the probability of a Type II error.

   d. Subtract the significance level from 1.0 to find the statistical power.

5. Which of the following statements is true about meta-analysis?

   a. Meta-analyses can be used as a basis for selecting a correlation in an a priori power analysis.

   b. Meta-analyses can help us develop practice guidelines from studies with diverse findings.

   c. Meta-analysis involves calculating the mean effect size across previously completed research studies on a particular topic.

d. All of the above.

e. None of the above.

6. Which of the following statements is true about meta-analysis?
   a. There is very little controversy about it.
   b. Because it is based on many studies it avoids coming up with misleading conclusions.
   c. The findings of studies with poor methodologies may be averaged in with findings from methodologically strong studies.
   d. It guarantees the avoidance of sampling bias.
   e. All of the above.

7. In selecting a test of statistical significance, we should consider:
   a. The level of measurement of the variables
   b. The number of variables included in the analysis
   c. The type of sampling methods used in data collection
   d. The way the variables are distributed in the population
   e. All of the above

8. Which of the following is *not* an assumption of parametric tests of significance?
   a. None of the variables has an interval or ratio level of measurement.
   b. The sampling distribution of the relevant parameters of the variables is normal.
   c. The different groups being compared have been randomly selected and are independent of one another.
   d. None of the above; they all are assumptions of parametric tests.

9. Which of the following is *not* a parametric test of significance?
   a. *t*-test
   b. Analysis of variance
   c. Chi-square
   d. Pearson's product-moment correlation

10. Which statistical test of significance should be used in a study of nominal data in a frequency distribution of ethnicity by whether or not the person is a school dropout?
    a. *t*-test
    b. Analysis of variance
    c. Chi-square
    d. Pearson's product-moment correlation

11. Which statistical test of significance should be used in a study of the relationship between number of children and years on welfare?

a. *t*-test
b. Analysis of variance
c. Chi-square
d. Pearson's product-moment correlation

12. Which of the following statements is *not* true about multivariate statistical analyses?
    a. If each of two variables, on a bivariate basis, separately accounts for 10% of the variation in a third variable, we can be certain that together they will account for 20% of the variation in the third variable.
    b. If two variables are correlated with each other, the amount of variation they both account for in a third variable will be less than the sum of their separate bivariate correlations with the third variable.
    c. Partial correlation coefficients measure the association between two variables after other, extraneous variables have been controlled.
    d. Multiple regression analysis shows the overall correlation between each of a set of independent variables and an interval- or ratio-level dependent variable.

13. Which of the following statements is true about inferential statistics?
    a. Failure to reject the null hypothesis means the same thing as verifying it.
    b. Rejecting the null hypothesis is a confirmation of the research hypothesis.
    c. When conducting multiple bivariate tests of significance we must adjust for the inflated probability of committing a Type I error.
    d. All of the above.

14. Which of the following statements is true about inferential statistics?
    a. All expert statisticians agree that statistical significance is irrelevant and misleading unless all of the assumptions of the chosen significance test have been met.
    b. Some statisticians prefer parametric tests of significance over nonparametric tests even when the characteristics of the variables being tested call for the use of nonparametric tests.
    c. There is very high agreement among statisticians that tests of significance can be applied to data gathered from an entire population rather than a sample.
    d. All of the above.

EXERCISE 17.1

Using Table 17.1 in the text, answer the following questions.

1. What sample size is needed to have statistical power exceeding .80:

a. Assuming a .05 significance level and a small effect size?

b. Assuming a .05 significance level and a medium effect size?

c. Assuming a .05 significance level and a large effect size?

d. Assuming a .10 significance level and a small effect size?

e. Assuming a .10 significance level and a medium effect size?

f. Assuming a .10 significance level and a large effect size?

2. What will your statistical power and probability of committing a Type II error be if your study:

a. Assumes a medium effect size, has a .05 significance level, and has a sample size of 30?

b. Assumes a medium effect size, has a .10 significance level, and has a sample size of 20?

c. Assumes a small effect size, has a .05 significance level, and has a sample size of 100?

d. Assumes a large effect size, has a .10 significance level, and has a sample size of 20?

EXERCISE 17.2

Suppose you wanted to conduct an experimental evaluation of an intervention to help parents of children with AIDS. Suppose further you are doing this in a small city, there is no way to find more than 40 sets of parents to participate in your study, and no other intervention with this target population is known to be effective. Discuss the adequacy of your statistical power. Would you use a .05 level of significance? Justify your answer in light of your use of Table 17.1 in the text. Explain why you would or would not choose to do the study, in light of your statistical power. Would your answer change if a previous pilot study had tentatively suggested that your intervention has very strong effects? Why or why not (in light of Table 17.1 in the text)?

EXERCISE 17.3

Suppose you are reviewing research to help you decide whether to use Intervention Approach A or Intervention Approach B to prevent high school dropout. You find only two studies. Study 1 found that in a community using Intervention Approach A, the dropout rate among the 5000 high-risk youths studied was 40%, while the rate in a comparable community that had no dropout prevention program was 45%. The difference was statistically significant. Study 2 randomly assigned 10 high-risk youths to Intervention Approach A and 10 high-risk youths to Intervention Approach B. The dropout rates were 40% for Approach A and 20% for Approach B, but the difference was not statistically significant. Which approach would you be inclined to use and to evaluate in your program, in light of the above data and the figures in Table 17.1 of the text? Why? (Include the concept of Type II errors in your answer.)

EXERCISE 17.4

Suppose you review a meta-analysis on the effectiveness of social work interventions in preventing high school dropout. It finds a mean effect size of .6 for intervention A, based on ten randomized experiments and five studies in which the group receiving the intervention was initially at higher risk of dropping out than the comparison group. The meta-analysis also finds a mean effect size of 1.5 for intervention B, based on a much larger number of studies, none of which were randomized experiments, and all of which used comparison groups that initially seemed to be at lower risk than the group receiving intervention B. Which of the two interventions would you be more inclined to use in light of this information? Why?

EXERCISE 17.5

Which test of statistical significance would you use for each of the following hypotheses? Why?

1. Students receiving intervention A are less likely to drop out of school than students receiving intervention B.

2. Students receiving intervention A will have fewer absences than students receiving intervention B.

3. Students receiving case management intervention will have fewer absences than students receiving a behavioral intervention, and students receiving the behavioral intervention will have fewer absences than students receiving supportive counseling.

4. The younger the student's mother, the more absences the student will have.

DISCUSSION QUESTIONS

1. Discuss the criteria that determine what test of statistical significance is most appropriate.

2. Suppose in bivariate correlations variable A accounts for 10% of the variance in a dependent variable, and variable B accounts for 10% of the variance in the same dependent variable, but variable A and variable B combined, in a multiple correlation, account for less than 20% of the variance in that dependent variable. Explain how this could be and illustrate it with overlapping circles.

3. Identify six common misuses or misinterpretations of inferential statistics and explain why each is a mistake.

4. Discuss both sides of the debate over whether it is appropriate to test the statistical significance of relationships found in data gathered from an entire population. Which side of the debate do you find more persuasive? Why?

CHAPTER

Program Evaluation

OBJECTIVES

1. Identify the similarities and differences between program evaluation research and other forms of social work research.
2. Discuss the historical development of program evaluation.
3. Describe the political aspects of program evaluation and their implications for objective scientific inquiry.
4. Compare the advantages and disadvantages of in-house evaluators and external evaluators.
5. Discuss political, ideological, and logistical factors that influence whether and how program evaluation is conducted or utilized.
6. Explain how evaluators can attempt to minimize stakeholder resistances to an evaluation and to maximize their utilization of it.
7. Describe alternative models of program evaluation and the advantages and disadvantages of each.
8. Describe quantitative and qualitative research methods used in process evaluations and in monitoring program implementation.
9. Discuss the functions of cost-effectiveness analysis and cost-benefit analysis and the complexities involved in them.
10. Discuss five alternative approaches to needs assessment and the advantages and disadvantages of each.
11. Differentiate the assessment of normative need and demand.
12. Identify the advantages and disadvantages of focus groups.
13. Discuss the ways quantitative and qualitative research methods can be combined in program evaluation.

PRACTICE-RELEVANT SUMMARY

Program evaluation has become ubiquitous in social work practice, as funding sources today demand evidence regarding the return on their investments in various programs and as human service professionals seek to find better ways to help people and do not want to see scarce welfare resources squandered on programs that don't really help their intended target populations. Funding sources often require a program evaluation component as a prerequisite for approving grant applications and supportive evaluative data as a basis for renewing funding. This requirement has been a mixed blessing. It has fostered more research that could help us improve policies and programs and find better ways to help people. But it also has politicized the evaluation research process, since the findings of evaluation research can provide ammunition to the supporters or opponents of a program.

Vested interests can jeopardize free, scientific inquiry. Pressure may be exerted to design the research or to interpret its findings in ways likely to make the program look good. Sometimes program evaluation is conducted in the cheapest, most convenient way possible, guided by the belief that funding sources don't care about the quality of the research; they just want to be able to say that the programs they fund have been evaluated.

In your social work practice you will probably participate in, conduct, or utilize many program evaluations. When you do, you should not be naive about the potential influence of vested interests on the integrity or quality of evaluations. At the same time, however, you should not become so overly cynical that you dismiss all program evaluation as politically biased. People with vested interests often have sufficient integrity and professional concern for learning the best ways to help clients that they are able to put their vested interests aside and act in a manner that fosters the most objective, scientific evaluation possible.

One factor thought to influence an evaluation's vulnerability to the biasing influences of vested interests is whether the program evaluation is conducted by evaluators who work for the agency being evaluated. When they do, they are called *in-house evaluators*. In contrast, *external evaluators* work for external agencies, such as governmental or regulating agencies, private research consultation firms, or universities. Despite their vulnerability to political pressure, in-house evaluators may have certain advantages over external evaluators, such as greater access to program information and personnel and more knowledge about the program, its research needs, and potential obstacles to the feasibility of certain evaluation designs. External evaluators also may be influenced by political considerations. In particular, they may want to get and stay in the good graces of the personnel of the program being evaluated, since those personnel often influence the decision about which external evaluators will be funded to conduct future evaluations of their services. Also, external sponsors of evaluations may be just as biased as in-house personnel. They may seek negative evaluation results to justify the cessation of funding of certain programs, or they may fret that negative results would make them (the sponsors) look bad and in turn threaten their own fundraising efforts. Whether or not program evaluation findings ultimately will be utilized often depends on whether they threaten or support deeply held beliefs or vested interests.

In addition to vested interests, another pragmatic factor influencing whether and how program evaluation studies are done is the logistics involved in their implementation. *Logistics* refers to getting subjects to do what they're supposed to do, getting research instruments distributed and returned, and other daily task details required to make a study feasible to carry out within the context of uncontrollable daily life in a particular agency. The logistical details of an evaluation project are often under the control of program administrators.

Steps have been suggested that program evaluators can take to prevent or minimize logistical problems and to promote the utility and ultimate use of their findings. To begin, they should learn as much as possible about stakeholders with vested interests in the evaluation. Evaluators should involve stakeholders in a meaningful way in planning the evaluation. Stakeholders include not only administrators and funders, but also service recipients and program personnel at all levels. Evaluators should share mutual incremental feedback with stakeholders throughout all phases of the evaluation. The cooperation of program personnel might be fostered further by assuring them that they will get to see and respond to a confidential draft of the evaluation report before it is finalized and distributed to other stakeholders. The evaluator can foster the utilization of the evaluation report by tailoring its form and style to the needs and preferences of those in a position to utilize it. Reports should be clear, succinct, cohesive, and carefully typed with a neat and uncluttered layout. When adapting the report to an audience of program personnel, do not present every peripheral finding and do not present negative findings bluntly and tactlessly. Couch negative findings in language that recognizes the yeoman efforts and skills of program personnel and that does not portray them as inadequate. Develop realistic, practical implications based on the findings.

While the foregoing steps are advisable, they are no guarantee that political or logistical pitfalls will be avoided. Your findings may be so negative that it is impossible not to threaten staff who are extremely fearful of losing precarious funding. When this happens, even if you follow all the recommended steps, stakeholders may still seek to discredit your evaluation. You may also find that the best-laid plans do not anticipate unforeseen logistical problems. Evaluation plans are unlikely to remain at the forefront of the minds of program personnel as they encounter unexpected difficulties in operating their programs and make program changes that impact the evaluation.

Program evaluation can have multiple purposes. It can assess the ultimate success of programs, problems in how programs are being implemented, or information needed in program planning and development. *Summative evaluations* are concerned with the first of the three purposes, involving the ultimate success of a program and decisions about whether it should be funded. *Formative evaluations* focus on obtaining information helpful in planning the program and in improving its implementation and performance. Summative evaluations will generally be quantitative in approach. Formative evaluations may use quantitative methods, qualitative methods, or both. These types or purposes of program evaluation are not mutually exclusive.

Evaluations of program outcome and efficiency may assess whether the program is effectively attaining its goals, whether it has any unintended harmful effects, whether its success is being achieved at a reasonable cost, and how the ratio of its benefits to its cost compares with the benefits and costs of other programs with similar objectives. This approach to evaluation is sometimes called the *goal attainment model of evaluation*. It involves operationally defining the formal goals of the program in terms of measurable indicators of program success, which serve as dependent variables in experimental and quasi-experimental designs that attempt to maximize internal validity within the feasibility constraints of the agency setting. The two major approaches to assessing the efficiency of a program are called cost-effectiveness analysis and cost-benefit analysis. In *cost-effectiveness analysis,* the only monetary considerations are the costs of the program itself; the monetary benefits of the program's effects are not assessed. In *cost-benefit analysis,* in addition to monetizing program costs, an effort is made to monetize the program's outcome.

The goal attainment model has been criticized by some for being overly concerned with formal goals, which are often stated in unreachable grandiose terms in order to secure funding or are stated so vaguely that different evaluators may not agree on how best to operationally define them. Evaluations focusing on a few operational indicators of success risk missing areas in which the program really is succeeding. Some argue that the evaluation of outcome therefore ought to be abandoned and replaced by evaluations of program processes. Others suggest keeping the goal attainment model but with some adjustments, such as measuring every conceivable indicator of outcome.

Some programs have unsuccessful outcomes simply because they are not being implemented properly. *Outcome evaluations* therefore should be supplemented by *evaluations of program implementation*. Evaluations of program implementation can have great value even without any evaluation of program outcome. If a program is not being implemented as planned, the need for changes may be implied without an outcome evaluation. But evaluations of program implementation are not necessarily concerned only with the question of whether a program is being implemented as planned. There are many other possible questions that examine how best to implement, as well as maintain, the program. Evaluations that focus on these questions are often called *process evaluations.* When programs are still in their infancy and have not yet had enough time to identify and resolve startup bugs and other problematic processes in implementation, outcome evaluations may be premature, and process evaluations may be more advisable. All of the methodologies covered in this book can be applied to evaluate program implementation. The most appropriate methodology to use depends on the nature of the research question. Although process evaluations can involve quantitative methods, they tend to rely heavily on qualitative methods such as open-ended qualitative interviewing or participant observation of staff or clients.

Evaluation also can be done before programs are implemented—for the purpose of program planning. The most common form of this type of evaluation is called needs assessment. *Needs assessment* studies may assess the extent and location of the problems the program seeks to ameliorate as well as the target population's characteristics, problems, expressed needs, and desires. This information is then used to guide program planning and development concerning such issues as what services to offer, how to maximize service utilization by targeted subgroups, where to locate services, and so on.

Needs can be defined in normative terms or in terms of demand. When defining needs *normatively*, needs assessments compare the objective living conditions of the target population with what society deems acceptable or desirable from a humanitarian standpoint. If needs are defined in terms of demand, however, only the individuals who indicate that they feel or perceive the need themselves would be considered to be in need of a particular program or intervention.

Five techniques for conducting a needs assessment are: (1) the key informants approach, (2) the community forum approach, (3) the rates under treatment approach, (4) the social indicators approach, and (5) the community survey approach. The *key informants approach* utilizes questionnaires or interviews to obtain expert opinions from individuals presumed to have special knowledge about the target population's problems and needs as well as about current gaps in service delivery to that population. The prime advantage of the key informants approach is that a sample can be obtained and surveyed quickly, easily, and inexpensively. The chief disadvantage of this method is that information is not coming directly from the target population; the quality of that information depends on the objectivity and depth of knowledge underlying the expressed opinions. The *community forum approach* involves holding a meeting in which concerned members of the community can express their views and interact freely regarding needs. The advantages of this approach include its feasibility, its ability to build support and visibility for the sponsoring agency, and its ability to provide an atmosphere in which individuals can consider the problem in depth and be stimulated by what others have said, thus taking into account things they might otherwise have overlooked. Its disadvantages include the questionable representativeness and objectivity of those who attend such meetings and of those who are the most vocal. The *rates under treatment approach* attempts to estimate the need for a service and the characteristics of its potential clients, based on the number and characteristics of clients already using that service in a comparable community. The prime advantages of the rates under treatment approach are its quickness, simplicity, low cost, and unobtrusiveness. Its prime disadvantage is that it assesses only the portion of the target population that is already using services, and thus it pertains primarily to demand and may underestimate normative need. Additional disadvantages would be involved if the comparison community provides the service in a way that potential consumers find undesirable or has unreliable or biased records and data. The *social indicators approach* examines aggregated statistics that reflect conditions of an entire population. Using social indicators is unobtrusive and can be done quickly and inexpensively, but there may be problems in the reliability of a particular existing database. The utility of this approach depends on the degree to which the existing indicators can be assumed to reflect future service utilization patterns accurately. The most direct way to assess the characteristics and perceived problems and needs of the target group is to survey its members, through the *community survey approach*. The advantages and disadvantages of the direct survey approach parallel those in surveys in general. Of particular concern is the need to have high response rates and minimize measurement biases such as those connected to social desirability and acquiescent response sets. Because each of the five approaches to needs assessment has its own advantages and disadvantages. Needs assessment studies ideally should combine two or more of the approaches to get a more complete picture of normative needs, felt needs, and demand for prospective services.

A qualitative research method often used for needs assessment, or for collecting other forms of program evaluation data, involves the use of focus groups, which consist of people who engage in a guided discussion of a specified topic. Focus group participants are typically chosen by means of purposive sampling or reliance on available subjects. They offer the advantage of being inexpensive, generating speedy results, and offering flexibility for probing. In addition, the group dynamics that occur in focus groups can bring out aspects of the topic that evaluators may not have anticipated and that may not have emerged in individual interviews. The disadvantages of focus groups include their questionable representativeness and the potential for group dynamics to create pressures for people to say things that may not accurately reflect their true feelings or their prospective actions. Another disadvantage is that the data emerging from focus groups are likely to be much more voluminous and less systematic than structured survey data. Analyzing focus group data, therefore, can be difficult, tedious, and subject to the biases of the evaluator.

A typology of three models of program evaluation practice has been proposed. The first model resembles the goal attainment model discussed earlier and holds that the greatest priority in program evaluation is to serve the public interest, not the interests of stakeholders who have vested interests in a program. Advocates of this model believe that summative evaluations, which test out whether programs really work—whether they are effective in delivering the public benefits they promise—are more important than finding out how and why they work. A second model posits that many solutions will be effective and that their effects will differ under different conditions. A program may be effective under certain conditions but may have opposite effects under different conditions. This model seeks to identify multiple variables that bear on differential program outcomes in different settings and emphasizes problems in the implementation. A third model focuses on serving the information needs of stakeholders. Rather than generalizing findings to other sites, this model restricts its focus to the particular program under study. In it the stakeholders (not the evaluator) play the key role in making decisions as to the design and purpose of the evaluation. Formative evaluations tend to be associated with this model.

REVIEW QUESTIONS

1. Which of the following statements is *not* true about program evaluation?
   a. It can apply qualitative as well as quantitative research methods.
   b. Although its rapid growth has been in the latter half of the 20th century, it dates back to earlier centuries.
   c. It is no more political than other forms of research.
   d. It is conceptually very similar to social work research.

2. Which of the following statements is true about program evaluation?
   a. It is always politically biased.
   b. It is almost never politically biased.
   c. Vested interests can impede the atmosphere for free, scientific inquiry.
   d. Funding sources always seek to obtain the most objective findings possible.

3. Which of the following is *not* an advantage of in-house evaluators (as compared to external evaluators)?

a. Greater knowledge of the program
b. Increased awareness of feasibility obstacles
c. Greater independence and objectivity
d. Greater likelihood of being trusted by program personnel

4. Which of the following statements is true about external evaluators?
   a. Future evaluation contracts are *not* influenced by the nature of the findings they report.
   b. Attacks on the credibility of their work are *not* motivated by the nature of the findings they report.
   c. Funding bodies sponsoring evaluations may have vested interests regarding the findings reported by the external evaluator.
   d. All of the above.
   e. None of the above.

5. In planning an evaluation, evaluators should:
   a. Minimize interaction with stakeholders who have vested interests in the outcome of the evaluation.
   b. Make sure stakeholders who have vested interests in the outcome of the evaluation are not involved in the planning of the evaluation.
   c. Keep program personnel, who ultimately might be one focus of the evaluation, out of the evaluation planning.
   d. All of the above.
   e. None of the above.

6. Summative evaluations of program success in goal attainment are more likely than other forms of evaluation to:
   a. Use experimental and quasi-experimental designs
   b. Use qualitative methods
   c. Be focused on the immediate informational needs of program administrators
   d. Ignore formal organizational goals

7. Which of the following statements is true about monitoring program implementation?
   a. Learning how well a program has been implemented can have an important bearing on the meaning of the results of a goal attainment evaluation.
   b. It may use quantitative as well as qualitative methods.
   c. It often involves process evaluation.

d. All of the above.

e. None of the above.

8. Which of the following statements is true about assessing the need for a particular program?

   a. The number of people who need a program may exceed the number who say they need it.

   b. The number who ultimately use the program will be accurately depicted by the number who say they will use it.

   c. We can be certain that the number of people who need a planned service in a community will be accurately depicted by the number who currently use the same service in a similar community.

   d. All of the above.

   e. None of the above.

9. In doing a cost-benefit analysis of a program:

   a. Complex principles of cost accounting are involved.

   b. We must go beyond purely economic considerations and must make value judgments about humanistic benefits.

   c. We ask whether monetized benefits exceed monetary costs.

   d. All of the above.

   e. None of the above.

10. Which of the following statements is true about the key informants approach to needs assessment?

    a. It utilizes experimental or quasi-experimental designs.

    b. Key informants are members of the target population, not practitioners.

    c. It is one of the most expensive, time-consuming approaches to needs assessment.

    d. A disadvantage is that the information is not coming directly from the target population.

11. Which of the following statements is true about the community forum approach to needs assessment?

    a. It utilizes rigorous survey designs.

    b. Its chief advantages are more pragmatic than scientific.

    c. Those who attend and speak at the forums have a high probability of being representative of the target population.

    d. It minimizes measurement bias.

12. Which of the following statements is true about the social indicators approach or the rates under treatment approach to needs assessment?
    a. The social indicators approach is obtrusive.
    b. The rates under treatment approach is obtrusive.
    c. The rates under treatment approach pertains primarily to demand and may underestimate normative need.
    d. The social indicators approach or rates under treatment approach ensures that the data are highly reliable.

13. Which of the following statements is true about the community survey or target group survey approach to needs assessment?
    a. It is an indirect way to assess need.
    b. It is the least expensive way to assess need.
    c. It is vulnerable to the disadvantage of low response rates or social desirability bias.
    d. If people say they will use a service, we can be very confident that they will use the service.

14. Which of the following statements is true about focus groups?
    a. They involve the use of quantitative research methods.
    b. Participants are typically chosen using probability sampling methods.
    c. Despite their advantages, they are expensive and time consuming.
    d. The group dynamics can bring out information that would not have emerged in a survey.

EXERCISE 18.1

Suppose you want to evaluate the effectiveness of a promising new form of child therapy to alleviate the harmful effects of traumatic experiences. To be certified to provide the new therapy, experienced practitioners must attend several weekend training workshops and ten sessions of monthly supervision. You arrange for half of the practitioners in a child guidance agency to obtain the training and supervision. Your plan is to see if the traumatized children assigned to the practitioners certified to provide the new therapy benefit more from treatment than comparable children assigned to the other practitioners.

1. What type of research design and measurement approach would you use to conduct the outcome evaluation?

2. What logistical problems would you be likely to encounter in implementing your design?

3. Who would be the stakeholders in your evaluation? What are their vested interests in the evaluation, and how might those vested interests potentially interfere with the rigor or implementation of your research design?

4. Identify the steps you would take to minimize resistance to the evaluation or the utilization of its results in the agency.

5. Describe how normative need versus demand might operate in assessing the need for the new therapy among children and their parents or guardians.

6. Discuss the importance of monitoring the implementation of the new service and how you would go about evaluating its implementation.

7. Discuss the difference in how you would evaluate the cost-effectiveness versus the cost-benefit of the new intervention. Identify difficulties in monetizing the benefits.

EXERCISE 18.2

Suppose you are a legislative aide specializing in social welfare policy for Senator Ginger Salamander. She is cautiously supportive of legislation to fund a series of expensive demonstration projects to test alternative ways to prevent child abuse, but only under the condition that each project be rigorously evaluated and that continued funding hinge on the evaluation findings. She envisions the funding going to the federal Office of Children bureaucracy, whose staff would administer the funding of the projects and of their evaluations. She asks you to advise her on the politics of program evaluation, how the politics may impact the evaluations, and how best to maximize the scientific integrity of the evaluation designs and their reports. What would you tell her, taking into account in-house versus external evaluators, vested interests, and the politics of evaluation? What would you recommend regarding her expectation that the federal bureaucrats will administer the evaluations?

EXERCISE 18.3

Conduct several qualitative, open-ended informal conversational interviews with other social work students about their satisfaction with the social work education program, its strengths, weaknesses, and needed improvements. Then engage the same students in a focus group discussion of the same topic. In what ways is the information generated by the two approaches similar and different?

EXERCISE 18.4

You are interested in starting a program to treat spouse abusers in an area that has not yet had such a program. But first you must document the need for the program, from a normative standpoint as well as from the standpoint of anticipating the likely level of utilization of the new program. Describe how you would assess this need, using each of the five approaches to needs assessment discussed in the text. Identify the advantages and disadvantages of each approach.

DISCUSSION QUESTIONS

1. Can all social work research be considered program evaluation research? Why or why not? If your answer is "no" identify, for discussion purposes, a social work research question that we would not be able to fit under the program evaluation rubric.

2. Do you think Chapter 18 of the Rubin and Babbie text is overly cynical about the corrupting influence of politics on program evaluation of outcome? Why or why not?

3. Do you agree with those who argue that evaluations should not focus on the attainment of formal organizational goals? Why or why not?

4. Do you prefer the stakeholder service model of evaluation practice? Why or why not? If not, which alternative model do you prefer, and why?

ANSWERS

Ch. 1	Ch. 2	Ch. 3	Ch. 4	Ch. 5	Ch. 6
1. e	1. d	1. d	1. e	1. b	1. d
2. f	2. c	2. f	2. d	2. c	2. c
3. e	3. a	3. d	3. c	3. b	3. b
4. c	4. b	4. c	4. e	4. a	4. a
5. e	5. a	5. b	5. d	5. c	5. d
6. d	6. b	6. d	6. b	6. a	6. a
7. e	7. a	7. c	7. c	7. b	7. c
8. b	8. c	8. c	8. a	8. c	8. b
9. c	9. a	9. e	9. b	9. a	9. d
10. a	10. b	10. b	10. d	10. d	10. f
11. b	11. a		11. b	11. f	11. d
	12. c		12. a		12. e

Ch. 7	Ch. 8	Ch. 9	Ch. 10	Ch. 11	Ch. 12
1. d	1. b	1. f	1. b	1. e	1. d
2. a	2. d	2. d	2. c	2. a	2. b
3. d	3. a	3. e	3. e	3. c	3. d
4. c	4. d	4. d	4. a	4. e	4. a
5. c	5. b	5. e	5. b	5. b	5. c
6. b	6. e	6. b	6. b	6. d	6. c
7. g	7. d	7. c	7. c	7. e	7. d
8. d	8. d	8. e	8. c	8. d	8. e
9. a	9. g	9. b	9. e	9. a	9. d
	10. b	10. a	10. e	10. a	10. d
	11. c	11. e	11. e		11. d
	12. b	12. e	12. e		12. b
		13. e	13. d		13. f
					14. a

Ch. 13	Ch. 14	Ch. 15	Ch. 16	Ch. 17	Ch. 18
1. e	1. d	1. a	1. a	1. f	1. c
2. a	2. b	2. b	2. d	2. d	2. c
3. f	3. e	3. c	3. d	3. a	3. c
4. a	4. d	4. d	4. e	4. b	4. c
5. c	5. a	5. c	5. b	5. d	5. e
6. d	6. a	6. a	6. c	6. c	6. a
7. b	7. a	7. b	7. a	7. e	7. d
8. f	8. d	8. a	8. d	8. a	8. a
9. c	9. d	9. a	9. c	9. c	9. d
10. a		10. d	10. e	10. c	10. d
		11. b	11. a	11. a	11. b
			12. c	12. c	12. c
			13. b	13. b	13. c
			14. c		14. d

To the owner of this book

I hope that you have enjoyed *Practice-Oriented Study Guide for Research Methods for Social Work, Third Edition* as much as I enjoyed writing it. I would like to know as much about your experience as you would care to offer. Only through your comments and those of others can I learn how to make this a better text for future readers.

School ______________________ Your instructor's name ______________________

1. What did you like the most about *Practice-Oriented Study Guide for Research Methods for Social Work, Third Edition*?

____

____

____

2. Do you have any recommendations for ways to improve the next edition of this text? __________

____

____

____

3. In the space below or in a separate letter, please write any other comments you have about the book. (For example, were any chapters or concepts particularly difficult?) I'd be delighted to hear from you!

____

____

____

____

____

____

Optional:

Your name ______________________ Date ______________________

May Brooks/Cole quote you, either in promotion for *Practice-Oriented Study Guide for Research Methods for Social Work, Third Edition,* or in future publishing ventures? Yes ☐ No ☐

Sincerely,

Allen Rubin

CUT ALONG DOTTED LINE

FOLD HERE

NO POSTAGE
NECESSARY
IF MAILED
IN THE
UNITED STATES

BUSINESS REPLY MAIL

FIRST CLASS PERMIT NO. 358 PACIFIC GROVE, CA

POSTAGE WILL BE PAID BY ADDRESSEE

ATTN: Allen Rubin

Brooks/Cole Publishing Company
511 Forest Lodge Road
Pacific Grove, California 93950-9968

FOLD HERE